# Nine Things

## Teens Should Know

### and Parents are Afraid to Talk About

9

D0682157

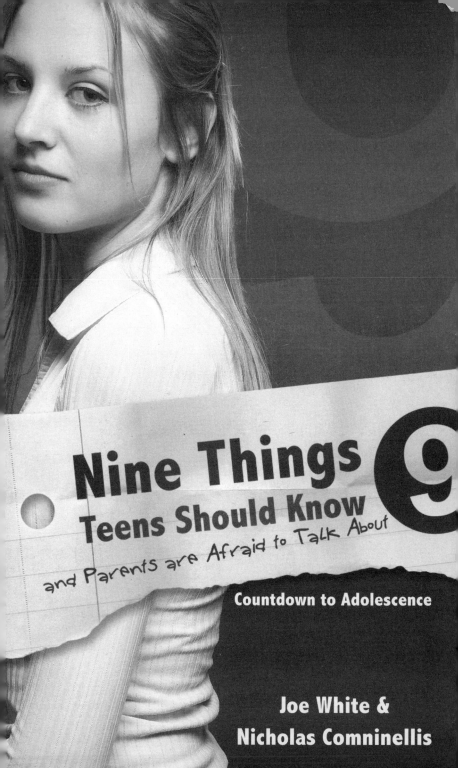

First printing: February 2006

ISBN-13: 978-0-89221-636-9
ISBN-10: 0-89221-636-0
Library of Congress Catalog Number: 2005936552

Cover and interior design:
Jayme Brandt, Twice Born, Eureka Springs, AR


**Printed in the United States of America**

For information regarding author interviews, please
contact the publicity department at (870) 438-5288.

Please visit our website for other great titles:
www.newleafpress.net

**New Leaf Press**
*A Division of New Leaf Publishing Group*

# Contents

# Foreword

Tucked into the beautiful Ozark Mountains — where I also happen to live — is one of the best-known "secrets" in the country.

I'm talking about Kanakuk Kamps, run by my good friend Joe White. A summer home to thousands of teens each year, Kanakuk reflects Joe's very large heart: full of love and compassion and understanding for new generations trying to find their place in the world. Outdoors activities are integrated with plenty of talk of values and faith. For years, parents have trusted Kanakuk and Joe White to be a positive, guiding force in the spiritual and social development of their children's lives and future.

Because of that, I'm very pleased to be able to recommend the latest book by Joe and his long-time co-author, Nicholas Comninellis. Joe and Nicholas are releasing *9 Things Teens Should Know And Parents are Afraid to Talk About.*

Nicholas, who volunteers much of his time at the Kamps each summer, and Joe have a desire to bring parents and their kids closer together — strengthening the family and its faith in a chaotic world where children are barraged with messages and temptations that can profoundly alter their lives in the worst of ways. At this critical stage of growing up, it can never be said too strongly how vital a strong foundation of faith and family support for these young people can be. The importance of faith and family is something I've built my own ministry on, so this new book was easy for me to absorb and get excited about. Designed to foster dialogue between parent and child, the book is easy to read and the many relevant applications will, I trust, make it an invaluable guide for parents who want to do a better job communicating with their teens — and vice versa! I believe this book will be an important guide for parents and an important bridge of communications to young people in addressing some of the most turbulent issues in society today.

I heartily recommend it; read it and be blessed.

Gary Smalley

Parents

# Preface For Parents

Adolescence is a critical time for both parents and their children. Your kids are rapidly moving toward adulthood and experiencing enormous physical, emotional, and social changes. Yet many obstacles lie between them and a successful transition. Your relationship with your kids is also developing new dimensions, which may add either closeness or great distance between the two of you.

When your child was an infant and toddler, he or she required constant physical care — hours on hours of feeding, bathing, dressing, and cuddling. As the years progressed, your role changed more toward encouraging intellectual and social development. You did homework together, pursued mutual hobbies, and arranged sleepovers with friends.

Now as an adolescent, more than ever, your child needs clear guidance. In a few short years, your child will be much more independent, immersed in the teen world — a world filled with hazards. Alcoholism, drug addictions, pregnancy, violence, law violations, and suicide are often the first ones that come to mind, but other hazards also abound: depression, physical injuries, parental conflicts, pornography (both the overt and subtle), and poor school performance.

Each year at Kanakuk Kamps in the mountains of Missouri and Colorado, Joe White and his staff host 20,000 kids in a transparent environment that fosters an amazing amount of open communication. One crying need among many teenage campers is how dearly they want to spend more time with their parents, how much they desire direction in life from Mom and Dad, and how they treasure the advice their parents can give — if they only would do so!

In medical practice, Dr. Nicholas Comninellis encounters multitudes of young people suffering the physical consequences of their misunderstandings about adolescence and the treacherous transition to adult life. They are often facing these crises alone because their parents are uninterested, too preoccupied, or completely absent.

You have a unique, once-in-a-lifetime opportunity to make a difference in your child's life. As he or she gets ready to enter the teen years, you likely have the last extended opportunity ever to give your children the knowledge and skills required for conversion to adult life.

You probably have your doubts, but as your child's parent, there is no one who is better qualified to guide them through this critical stage. No one else knows your child's character like you do. You've lived with them for years. No one else loves your child as ferociously as you do. You've sacrificed vast quantities of sleep, energy, and money on their behalf. No one has a stronger interest in your child's success than you do. You're willing to give whatever it takes to see them prosper in life. In spite of their mood swings and phases of resistance, after counseling countless adolescents we are convinced that parents hold the keys to a child's heart like no other human being on earth.

## GIVING UP AT HALFTIME

In spite of these truths, most parents don't talk to their children about anything more than the superficial issues of daily life: their schedules, homework, and household chores. It's no wonder, then, that such kids are more likely to encounter problems as adolescents — problems with potentially devastating consequences.

By guiding your child through this stage of life, you both prepare him or her for success, and help to protect yourself from profound disappointments. James Dobson, president of Focus on the Family, explains:

> The primary reason adolescence is so distressing is because youngsters do not fully understand what is happening to them. Many of their fears and anxieties and discouragements could be obviated by a simple instructional program.[1]

Yet where is the program? Where are the parents? In particular, where are the fathers? The average father of a teenager will only spend three and a half minutes a day talking with his son, but will spend about 40 hours a week working, 50 hours sleeping, and 7 hours dressing and grooming.

Multiplied over a lifetime, you can see the problem. The average father spends 25 years sleeping, 12 years working, 3 years grooming, and only 11 days and 16 hours talking to his son or daughter. A survey in a teen magazine found that only four and a half percent of America's teenage girls felt that they could go to their father with a serious problem. Is this any wonder, given the little investment most fathers make into their kids' lives?

## SECOND-RATE COACHES

Lacking the active input of parents, children are going elsewhere to learn about adolescence and the "adult world." Just where are they looking?

First of all, they turn to their peers — especially those who are a year or two older. While your child may be fortunate to have a teenage mentor who will point him or her in the right direction, getting reliable guidance from another teen is quite a gamble. Your child might get lucky, but the odds are remote. Chances are that he or she will wind up following an older peer who has far less insight than you would ever choose.

Another major source of education about teen life is television and movies, but like finding a reliable teen mentor, this investment has an extremely low yield. Instead of viewing something enlightening, by the time the average teenager is 18, he or she will see over 18,000 murders on television. Of the 50,000 to 100,000 sexual encounters that a typical teen will see on TV, over 92 percent are in pre-marital or extra-marital relationships. This should come as absolutely no surprise. Surveys of

Hollywood's most influential TV writers and producers consistently demonstrate their support of "realistic" violence and pre-marital sex, while also confirming their disdain for anything moral, much less religious.

No wonder Bing Crosby observed, "Writers and producers are working nudity, permissiveness, irresponsibility, profanity, scenes of semi-explicit sex, provocative dialogue, smutty innuendoes and situations into their shows. . . . I fear they are depicting life as it is going to be if they are not diverted." These media moguls are the very people who create the videos our teenagers are entertained with an average of three to four hours a day!

A third incredibly powerful influence on children is music. Just look at the CD collection and stereo equipment that many of them possess! Notice how children are attracted to pop music's star performers. Recognize the number of hours a day they spend bathing in the rhythms and their messages. The typical teen spends over two hours a day plugged in! That's a minimum of 75,000 songs between the ages of 13 and 19.

What are these songs about? You may be shocked when you take the time to read the lyrics. The most perverted, profane, degenerate blitz of information to ever infiltrate the minds of youth is exactly what's found in most of the top-selling popular music: messages of lawlessness, unfaithfulness, raw sex, homosexuality, murder, and suicide.

### Games, Internet?

Lacking your personal guidance, the alternative influences over your child in this susceptible time are quite often deadly. Peer pressure prowls your neighborhood and schools like a street gang looking for a new recruit. The media bombards your child with perverted role models who dare, "Come live like me!" All the while, popular music is chanting the most perverted of all messages, enticing your child to give in.

## TWO-MINUTE WARNING!

As adolescence is beginning to dawn, a growing number of parents are waking up and committing themselves to prepare their kids. These parents accept the challenge to train them and to equip them in spite of fatigue, time restraints, and uncertainty.

The courage and conviction of these parents — parents like you — is admirable. What they often lack, however, is a tool to help them begin. What do kids most need to know about adolescence? How can it be explained? What questions most perplex them? Which answers are most helpful?

The purpose of this book is to help communicate the vital information pre-teens both desire and require. While reading alone will be profitable for your child, the experience will be much more effective if you discuss the topics together. For this reason, we encourage you to take time to read *Nine Things Teens Should Know* for yourself.

Make time to ask your child for his or her thoughts, feelings, or opinions on what they are reading in this book. Make the experience as interactive as possible. You may also find that recounting stories from your own adolescence will both make your child feel at ease and help to enhance the discussions you have together.

You may feel uncomfortable discussing some subjects, especially those related to sex and relationships. Most of us remember the discomfort we ourselves felt when our own parents tried to talk with us about similar matters. But don't worry too much! A degree of anxiety is normal. You may even want to diffuse the situation by sharing with your child the anxiety you are feeling.

As you talk, also take time to express your affection for your kid. Point out and compliment their successes, aspirations, energy, imagination, and dreams. The truths contained in this book, along with your personal affirmation, can combine to make the experience of preparing for adolescence one your child will treasure, and one that will bring the two of you closer together.

Each chapter of *Nine Things Teens Should Know* is divided into three sections for easier comprehension:

 • *Getting to the Core.* This is the essential information about the subject of the chapter.

 Stories that relate are also intermingled. Feel free to share your own similar experiences as you talk with your kid about the chapter.

 • *What Do You Think?* These are personal application questions the reader can consider alone. Or better yet, the two of you can discuss your responses together.

 • *For Teen Eyes Only.* This contains a challenge for teens to take action on the subject. At the end of each chapter, be sure to ask your kid what decision or conclusion he or she reached about the subject.

Adolescence is different for each child. For this reason, the content of this book must be general in nature. If you feel at some point that your child's development or behavior may be peculiar, worrisome, or abnormal be sure to consult a professional. Talking with your child's physician, school guidance counselor, youth group leader, or mental health consultant may be an excellent resource for assistance.

## GOAL

This time investment you make into your kid is one of the wisest of all parental choices. With the right preparation, the incredibly dangerous environment your teen enters can become one that brings out the best in them, especially against the backdrop of their confused and distraught peers. Preparing your child for adolescence can also be an experience that brings out the very best in you; one that demonstrates your own foresight, dedication, and true love.

If you plant a tree in an open field where the wind blows and light comes from every angle, chances are that it will only grow short and round. If you plant a sapling in a dense forest where the trees are erect and the light comes from above, chances are good this small tree will grow tall and straight. It can be exactly the same with your child. The combination of good role models and clear direction will inspire your teen to grow up with wisdom, strength, and stature.

The pressure is on. The game is almost over. Help your child prepare for the scrimmages of adolescence. In just a few short years, yours can be the great satisfaction of seeing an 18-year-old son or daughter win the game, having victoriously passed though the most tumultuous period of a life!

Notes

1. James Dobson, *Hide or Seek* (Old Tappan, NJ: Fleming H. Revell Co., 1974), p. 108.

# Teens

**Nine Things Teens Should Know**

# Preface For Teens

Growing up is all about change and development. If you've owned pets, you've witnessed firsthand how they transform from playful, clumsy babies to assured, mature adults. If you have siblings, you can't help but observe how their interests have altered from, say dolls, to friends, and then to boyfriends or girlfriends. No doubt you've also noticed the physical transformation among your buddies and classmates. Year by year, they become taller, smarter (hopefully), and more athletic than before.

Certainly you're aware that your own body is changing. You may have noticed that your clothes are tighter or shorter than they used to be, you're switching shoe sizes every few months, or you're starting to discover body hair in unusual places.

What's more, you're likely aware that your interests are on the move. You're not attracted to the style of clothes that once appealed to you. Your pet animals may not be as entertaining anymore. You may not be as interested as before in hanging out with your brothers or sisters. Your preference in friends has altered, so that some who once seemed fun aren't so much anymore, and vice versa.

You are entering a very special stage of life called adolescence. It's the final step — the final quarter — between being a child and becoming a fully developed adult. Adolescence involves changes that affect almost every part of your life, including your body, your emotions, your relationship with your parents, your interaction with friends, and your goals and dreams for the future.

Adolescence is a stage filled with enormous ideas and energy. It can be by far the most exciting, wonderful experience of your life to date. It can also be a time filled with self-doubt, depression, and anxiety — a phase you agonize through almost everyday.

Consider the plight of Chris:

> Sixth grade was an extremely tough year. I was attending a new elementary school where the boys were bigger and liked to push me around at the bus stop. I was having trouble reading, and got put into a special education class. At one point I became covered with poison ivy, and had to sit in an isolated corner of the room, from where the other kids jeered me. "Touch him and you'll get infected," they'd call to one another.
>
> Embarrassing black hair started growing on my legs, and then on my upper lip. I'd sneak into my parent's bathroom and scrape the nasty black stuff off of my face with a razor, cutting myself in the process. A short time later, friends invited me to a pool party. It was then that I faced one of the greatest dilemmas of my youth: should I shave the

**Nine Things Teens Should Know**

black hair off my legs before I go? Questions plagued me. What would my friends say if they discovered how burly I really was? What if I cut myself again and had to get stitches? In the end, I just told my friends I couldn't go, but I felt terrible for days about missing the fun I should've had with them.

Then there was Stacy. Every time I saw her, these incredibly wild emotions exploded within me. We'd play dodge ball together at recess and I'd come back into school feeling like a million bucks. We'd be picked to raise the flag in front of our school, and I'd come in flying like a kite. The day Stacy pressed a love letter into my hand I must have soared to a thousand feet, but a few days later Stacy told me to "flake off" and I felt as though I had crashed into a million pieces.

The year reached a crisis one afternoon when I got home from school. Suddenly I began crying. I don't know why, I just felt like it. I cried my heart out, wailing and all. The sobs brought my mother scurrying from the yard.

Alarmed at my tears, she put her arms around me and urged, "Honey, what's wrong?"

"You really want to know?" I replied sarcastically, pulling away. So I unloaded on her about the irritating bigger boys, the "special" reading class, the hairy epidemic infecting my body; and yes, even my infatuation with Stacy.

At first my mother looked very worried, like I might have become a mental case or something.

When I finally finished describing my plight, she took on a look of reassurance. "Chris, don't worry," she sighed. "You're just going through adolescence."

"Ado-what?" I replied. "Whatever you call it, I don't like it!" I shook my head firmly.

"Chris," Mom continued, "adolescence is just a normal part of growing up. Let's talk about it some more."

My mom started opening up to me about what she went through as a kid, about her embarrassing moments and struggles to find true friends. I discovered she had been through much of the same stuff I was feeling. She even helped me figure out how to deal with my hair and what to do next time I saw Stacy. I felt so glad we could talk like this.

## COACHING THE FINAL QUARTER

Parents, teachers, and youth pastors are like the coaches of a sports team. Their job is to prepare the players for real competition. They start by teaching the fundamentals of the game. Next, they train players in the more complex strategies of winning. Along the way, coaches instruct the athletes how to play fair, avoid injuries, and deal with unexpected turns in the game. It's not just theory they are trying to get across, but actual skills essential for real play.

That play gets particularly rough in the final quarter. The competition is vigorous, the team is easily frustrated, the goal is only yards away, and the clock keeps ticking. Adolescence is like that. There's so much to learn, so many experiences to try out, and so little time in which to accomplish it all.

## ADOLESCENT GAME PLAN

For victory in the final quarter, you must have great coaches, but even coaches need a playbook — one that spells out the sure-fire strategies for success. Someone gave you this book because they have your best interests at heart. They want you to enjoy adolescence and take advantage of all the great adventures it can bring. They want to see you shine during these years, and carry that shimmer with you into adulthood. The discoveries you make while reading this book will help you become a happier, stronger, more confident person. The truths you'll encounter in these pages will also catapult you miles ahead of your peers, many of whom will have to figure out the secrets of adolescence on their own.

I (Joe) wobbled through the difficult years of elementary to junior high school with an embarrassment that would not go away: two giant silver front teeth. A sports accident cost me half of my two front teeth that had to be capped with chrome. My summer camp counselor called me "Grill Face," like my face was the front end of a car. As if I didn't feel awkward enough over my looks, trying to keep up with ever-changing hair styles, clothing styles, and fighting for a starting position on the football and basketball teams, my teeth made me feel every day like I was just trying to survive. This book could have definitely helped me get through those tough years!

## Body by Design

As surely as a meager caterpillar develops inexpressibly into a majestic butterfly, all living creatures were designed by God with a life cycle; certain stages of development that the creature goes through as a normal part of existence. It is no different in the case of humans.

Between a newborn baby and fully developed adult lie a multitude of physical, emotional, and social changes. Adolescence is a period of time during which these changes happen the fastest. For boys, this stage usually begins around 10–12 years of age. To most boys chagrin, girls start sooner, and 9–10 is more the norm. In either case, the intense experience of adolescence can be expected to last five or six years. With all the changes that must take place, your mind and body will be very busy during this time span.

Occasionally, like Chris did, young people sometimes equate adolescence with some kind of disease. It is true that this stage of life is accompanied by some striking physical and emotional upheavals, but be assured, these are entirely normal. Adolescence is as natural a part of life as a baby learning to walk or a kid throwing a ball.

In the following chapters we'll investigate some of the biggest changes and issues that happen during adolescence. We'll look into:

- Emotional changes — how your mind learns to deal with new experiences.
- Romantic feelings — the way your heart responds to your natural attraction for those of the opposite sex.

- Social life — the new patterns of interacting with people of your own age.

- Substance abuse — how to resist the temptations which can lead to drug and alcohol addiction.

- Media influence — ways to take control over what you watch and listen to.

- Parental relationships — getting along better with your mom and dad.

- Physical changes — the way your body prepares itself for adulthood.

- Self-esteem issues — feeling good about who you are and where you're going in life.

Each chapter of *Countdown To Adolescence* is divided into three sections to help you make the most of your read:

- *Getting to the Core.* This is the essential truth about the subject.

- *What Do You Think?* These are some questions to consider that might help you to apply the core information.

- *For Teen Eyes Only.* This last section contains a challenge for you to reach a decision or to take a stand, one that will make you proud!

Your parents may be reading this book along with you. They may want to talk with you about it, or even share some of their own experiences with adolescence.

This may make you feel uneasy, but give your parents a chance. They really can help make the whole process of growing up more trouble-free and enjoyable.

You may breeze over some of the hurdles of adolescence with barely a bump. Others may seem too high to ever pass over, but do not lose heart. While adolescence is a challenging period in life, you can enjoy this stage like none before, and emerge on the other side totally prepared to take on the exciting adult world!

"...in adolescence the **ups and downs are greater** than at any other time **during your life.**"

# Chapter

**1**

# Crazy Emotions

## GETTING TO THE CORE

The physical changes of adolescence are striking, but even more remarkable are the changes that will occur inside your head. As an adolescent, you experience some feelings that are entirely new to you. You also experience familiar feelings, but with more intensity than you ever imagined.

Adolescents tend to feel stronger about almost everything—regardless of the subject. Joys seems greater. Disappointments feel deeper. Friendships are more cherished. Adversaries are more disdained. Sometimes you feel extremely scared or incredibly proud. Other times you feel terribly sad or explosively exuberant. You also may not be sure exactly what you are feeling, only that, whatever it is, the sensation is overwhelming! The fear of sudden rises and falls of your first roller coaster ride is nothing compared to some of the emotional peaks and valleys you face.

Together, we're going to explore some of the most common emotional experiences of young people. It's helpful to be familiar with these feelings in advance. This way, when they happen you won't be surprised, and you may even be able to take better advantage of your tremendous emotional energy.

## SOMETIMES UP, SOMETIMES DOWN

Everyone's emotions naturally fluctuate, but in adolescence the ups and downs are greater than at any other time during your life. Occasionally, you go through periods of feeling certain that you are worthless; that no one anywhere really loves you; that there is nothing to anticipate in life but depression. Don't worry — these feelings are not at all permanent!

Josh, age 14, explains the experience:

> You never know what life's going to throw at you. You can be really happy one day, and the next feel like nothing could go more wrong. A lot of times I wake up in the morning and things seem so perfect. I make it to the bus on time and my classes are going great. Then all it takes is one person to say one thing negative to me, and my day is ruined! It works the opposite way, too. A friend will say one little good thing like, "You're really good at acting," or "I like your T-shirt," and all of a sudden I'm feeling wonderful. It helps me to be ready for these ups and downs so I don't feel so devastated by them.

Like Josh, you will also go through stages when you will feel like the entire world is on your side; like you're the luckiest boy or girl in the world; like happiness, peace, and love are everywhere. You'll experience incredible giddiness, energy, and joy.

Regardless of how you are feeling at any instant, it will soon change, guaranteed. If you are riding high on a wave of satisfaction, within a few days or weeks you will probably begin to come down again. If you are experiencing the lowest of lows, in just a short time your emotions will almost always begin to change for the positive.

Swings between times of happiness and sadness are a normal part of being a youth. It's important to realize this fact for two special reasons. First, so that you don't do anything you will later regret while you're at one extreme or another. While in depression, some teens run away from home, get into trouble with the law, turn to drugs and alcohol, or even commit suicide. If they realized that their depression was only a phase they were going through, they might not have made such senseless choices. By just waiting a short time, their emotions would inevitably have perked up.

It's also helpful to use the nature cycle of emotions in planning your activities. When you are in a high-energy phase, it may be a very good time to complete some difficult school assignments, finish an organizing project at home, or other activity that requires creativity and endurance. On the other hand, when you realize you're in a low-energy phase, it may be best to put off challenging jobs that can wait until later. By being aware of your emotional cycles,

**Nicholas Comninellis & Joe White**

you can adjust your activities to match your mood and avoid some frustrations.

Some responsibilities, unfortunately, can't be postponed. Just as your parents likely have a job that they don't totally enjoy all the time, they still get up and go to work when they are expected. They still fulfill their responsibilities once on the job. It's the same for youth. You may be feeling low energy, and not especially interested in your classes or extracurricular activities, but it is your "job" to do your best in spite of your emotional state. Besides, positive activity and accomplishments are one of the greatest remedies for gloominess.

Remember that emotional swings are not confined to adolescence. You'll experience them throughout your life. If you learn to handle them now, you'll have a big advantage over most other teenagers, and many adults, too. Like driving a car or typing, managing your emotional energy is a skill you will use almost every day of your life. The sooner you master it, the more prepared you'll be for life.

## NOT ALL AS IT SEEMS

Closely related to fluctuating emotions is a second fact you should be aware of: the unreliability of first impressions, and dangers of being impulsive. All of us, when we meet a new person or encounter new situations, draw conclusions about them: whether the person is trustworthy or the situation is safe, for example. A particular challenge in adolescence is that new situations and first impressions are extremely common. Sometimes your initial impressions will be absolutely correct, but other times you'll completely miss the mark.

Josh puts it this way:

> Nobody shows you who they really are at first. No one wants to trust complete strangers, because they are afraid that you won't like them. Instead, they just show you how cool they are or what they want you to see, even if that's not who they really are. You really need to get to know people before you can trust them.

The problem is that our emotions distort or change the true picture of what is happening around us. If you act upon your initial impulses, you can find yourself in deep predicaments. If you fall in love with a person you just met and try to get too close to him or her, you could easily get slapped! If you feel rage and strike another person, it could put you in trouble with the police. If you get frustrated during a sports team practice and decide to just quit, you may ruin the chance for wonderful athletic victories.

Jesse was in eighth grade when he began looking for a bass player to play in his garage band. Like drummers, good bass players were hard to find, especially someone who already knew the songs Jesse liked. He talked it up at school and then posted a note online. That's when Peter called. Peter was a couple of years older and from a different school district, but Jesse downloaded some songs he'd played on and was impressed. Besides, Jesse had a gig in

just two weeks and was feeling pressure to cancel unless he had someone to play bass.

Jesse told the other guys in the band how excited he was to finally have a bass player. Everyone expressed relief that this obstacle was finally out of the way. Then Peter showed up at band practice with his flashy guitar and effects processor, further impressing Jesse. Peter even played his parts okay. Jesse reassured the host of the party where his band was playing that they'd be ready to play.

With their performance only days away, Jesse's band was rehearsing almost every afternoon. Peter usually showed up, but arrived later and later each time. Jesse also noticed Peter's clothes smelled weird, and he seemed more and more disinterested in the music. One afternoon, just two days away from their show, Peter was looking especially glassy eyed. Instead of tuning up his instrument, he slouched on the couch, pulled out a marijuana cigarette, and lit it with a match.

"Hey, why all the pressure, guys," said Peter. "Let's take it easy for a change. Come share this joint with me."

Jesse didn't know what to say. "Hey, Peter, we're here to play music. Not to get high! Why do you think I asked you to join our band?"

"Well, sure, I want to play music, too," replied Peter in a disinterested voice, "but the real reason I joined was to find some people to smoke pot with me."

There is a way to get around the inaccuracies of first impressions: give them time. Time has a way of giving us real experience, allowing our emotions to calm down, of giving our minds a chance to think, of helping us to discern good and evil, right and wrong, better and best. Don't ignore strong initial impressions, but be very careful about acting upon them until you have time to sort them out. Learn to recognize the difference between an impulse and a well-thought-out idea.

## GIVE ME SOME SPACE!

When you were an infant, you needed constant attention from your parents; someone to dress you, bathe you, feed you, and all the rest. As you became stronger and more coordinated, you began to demand, "I can do it myself!" You insisted on playing your own games, reading your own books, and choosing your own foods to eat. With time, you developed talents, likes, and dislikes that were uniquely "you."

By the time you reach adolescence, you feel pretty comfortable in your ability to care for yourself. You also want even more independence in your decisions than ever before: the right to set your own bedtime, to wear whatever you want, and do your homework when you see fit. Along with this freedom, you want more physical space: your own room, stereo, telephone, and so on. You also want "emotional space" — the freedom to choose when and where you express your private thoughts to others.

You likely feel increasing embarrassment about being around your parents or siblings in public, especially when that "public" includes your friends. At times, this emotion can be so strong you would rather just stay at home than risk being seen with them.

Rachel's need for space became especially obvious one evening during eighth grade. She was in charge of a youth meeting at church. On the surface, the job was pretty easy. She would just get up in front, welcome everyone, read the announcements, and then lead the singing. What was nerve-wracking was the fact that almost all of Rachel's best friends were in the crowd. Before leaving home for the meeting she'd rehearse her lines, memorize the songs, and make sure her jeans looked just right.

One evening as Rachel was anxiously getting ready, her mother suddenly popped her head in the door. "Rachel, I'm going to drop your little brother and sister off at the meeting with you tonight." She smiled, and turned to walk away.

"But Mom!" Rachel gasped in sudden anguish, "you can't do that!"

"Well, why not, Honey?" her mother replied innocently. "I've got to go grocery shopping and they won't want to come."

"But all my friends will be there! Please don't do this to me!" Rachel's previous anxiety over leading suddenly paled in comparison to the embarrassment of being seen with her siblings.

"What's the big deal?" her mother persisted. "Is there something wrong with your brother and sister?" She was becoming defensive.

"Well, no," Rachel sheepishly replied, "they're all right. It's just . . . I just don't think this meeting is right for them, being younger than me, you know."

Her mother's expression began to wise up. "No Rachel, I think there's more to this than you're admitting."

Rachel's mother was right to a degree. The group was an important part of Rachel's social identity outside of home. It was her personal "space" — one Rachel was understandably reluctant to share with her family. Rachel's mother needed to learn to be sensitive to this fact, and to learn to ask before invading her social space. All in all, the move toward greater social independence is healthy for you. Someday you'll be living on your own, choosing your own friends, studies, jobs, vacations, and hobbies. The experience and step-by-step independence you develop now is essential for the coming phases of life.

- What kind of things happen that make you feel especially sad or happy?
- What sort of activities do you enjoy more when you are feeling up?
- What do you do to help yourself survive the down times?
- Why is it important to not make big decisions when you are feeling down or extremely happy?
- What do your parents do that invades your personal space?
- What do you need to do to help your parents understand your need for privacy?

## FOR TEEN EYES ONLY

You will likely find that adolescents, including yourself, tend to analyze almost everything they were taught as children. Kids usually grow up using the values instilled in them by their parents. If their parents are prejudiced against other races, chances are their children will be prejudiced also. If their parents express faith in God, it's likely that their children will, too. If their parents value fine cars (or football, liquor, snow skiing, gourmet food, or any number of other things), chances are the kids will also desire those pleasures.

In the teenage years, you will find yourself completely re-evaluating the concepts and values you learned while growing up. This period of reassessment is very likely accompanied by feelings of insecurity and uneasiness. No surprise! Just when you thought you knew what was true and untrue, right and wrong, the facts become blurry. Your sense of peace and happiness undergoes a massive shake-up, and you feel like confusion reigns in your life.

Victoria is a high school girl who comes to our Kanakuk sports camps each summer. She's incredibly motivated, content, and enthusiastic about life, but it was not always this way. Listen to her story:

> My parents are wonderful. As I grew up, they've loved me, shared their dreams with me, and gave me the chance to do all sorts of extracurricular activities. I knew what I believed about God, about sex, about morals. I even knew what career I wanted to pursue.
>
> When I hit my sophomore year in high school, all that changed. I suddenly found myself resisting my parent's values. I stopped going to church. I started reading books about strange ideas. I discovered heavy metal rock. My school grades went to the ground floor. I found new friends, wild friends — the kind I would never have been attracted to before. My motivation and dreams for competitive swimming evaporated.
>
> Along with all the questions I was asking, I felt this terrible unhappiness. I cried a lot.

**Nicholas Comninellis & Joe White**

I'd spend hours in my room just staring at the walls. I even thought about suicide, though I'd never actually do it. My parents were worried about me, really worried. In fact, they even sent me to a counselor, but nothing anyone could do helped.

That school year seemed like it was never going to end, but as the months passed, I found myself thinking again about what I believed as a child. It's like, I needed that chance to go outside the comfortable little world I was raised in, and just see what I really thought about life.

Gradually, I started coming out of my room. I lost interest in those wild friends. I talked to my coach about rejoining the swim team. I even started going back to church again.

The best part is that along with this "re-entry" I also experienced that former peace and contentment returning to me. I felt like I'd spent a year in the desert, and finally I was coming back home, but I was coming home by my own choice. Not because I had to. It was my own decision.

As a kid, you tend to take things at face value. Life seems pretty simple. As you move toward being an adult, you will naturally question and reassess the ideas you learned growing up. Confusion will periodically seem to reign in your life — a consequence of this reassessment, but don't lose hope. Reassessment is, all in all, a very important process. Reassessment is how the values you grew up with actually become your OWN personal values. Without this process, you'll be simply living your parent's values. Only as you reassess can you actually make them uniquely yours and become your own unique person.

"...I began to sweat,
I felt both nervous and excited.
and I just couldn't wait to be
closer..."

**9** **Nine Things**
Countdown to Adolescence

## Chapter

**2**

# "I Think I'm In Love"

### GETTING TO THE CORE

Todd's sixth grade year began like he expected —new teachers, new books, and new friends. There awaited another experience that took him by complete surprise—a new girl. Todd had never in his life seen such a beautiful person, and she was in his own classroom! Donna had curly dark hair and an unspeakably enticing smile. She seemed to float, not walk; to sing, not speak.

Todd describes his experience:

I could hardly keep my mind off of Donna. Between classes we'd hang out by her locker. In reading class we passed notes back and forth. Before long, we were talking over the phone for hours each night. Virtually everything about Donna enchanted me. You know, in grade school guys didn't hang out with girls much. They were just somehow inferior to boys, but Donna was so different. She just completely changed my ideas about girls.

If love were a disease, Todd was in desperate need of a doctor. "Being in love" was unmistakably his diagnosis! Todd continued:

During those first few weeks with Donna I had no idea what was happening to me, or even that what I felt had a name. All I knew is that every time I saw Donna my heart jumped, I began to sweat, I felt both nervous and excited, and I just couldn't wait to be closer to her. My friends began to whisper, "You've got a crush!" You know what? They were absolutely right!

My (Joe's) youngest daughter Courtney had a crush on her sixth grade boyfriend, Ross, a guy not much different from Todd. They "went out" three times (never actually going anywhere) and "broke up" three times in three months. Crazy thing about it was, they never even spoke to each other! All the "go outs" and "break ups" happened via communication with each other's best friends!

Becoming interested in the opposite sex is a highlight of adolescence. Suddenly, the girls who used to be ignored because they were somehow "contagious" become the center of attention. The boys who were formerly simply "stupid," suddenly become "so handsome and talented."

The two sexes who used to avoid one another at almost all costs are now inseparable.

One by one, you'll find both your friends and yourself "falling in love." The word "fall" is appropriate here, because the experience is often one of feeling out of control, overcome by powerful emotions that may border on ecstasy or insanity, or both.

## GOD'S WIRING

The first few times you "fall in love" you may believe something terribly abnormal is happening, but don't worry! This incredible attraction was designed by God. He intended for us to be captivated with one another, and this captivation goes into high gear in your adolescent years.

This attraction is sometimes called a "sexual appetite," and is as natural as your desire for food and for sleep. It's a normal part of being a human. On the highest level, sexual attraction is one of the forces that draws men and women to date, to marry, to enjoy a sexual relationship, and to eventually create children of their own.

Sure, you are years away from marrying, but in adolescence you begin to experience a passion to be with people of the opposite sex. Some of this drive results from the encouragement of your friends, or even from your parents, but most of it has to do with normal chemicals in your body called hormones. Once these special hormones start sending out messages to your brain, it's almost impossible to ignore the opposite sex.

Boys usually find themselves mesmerized by girl's bodies; the way they are built, their curves, the softness of their skin, the reflection of light on their hair. Girls, by contrast, are not quite so excited over the shape of a boy's body. They are more charmed by the boy himself; his personality, his laugh, his ideas, and humor.

A crush is what happens when this attraction hits its emotional peak. The word "infatuation" is also a very apt description. You feel like everything in your body is turbocharged and pumped up. You find yourself thinking about, and obsessing over, the person almost all the time. You look for chances to see him or her, or excuses to call on the phone. You daydream about being together. You find it hard to sleep or concentrate on sports or home-work. When you are around him or her, you usually feel nervous or excited beyond words.

Sometimes the desire to express a crush will come rushing out of you like a massive crowd exiting the school during a fire alarm. When my (Joe's) son Cooper played his first junior high basketball game in a nearby town, the entire female student body of the opposing team became mesmerized by his looks and began chanting his name. If that wasn't embarrassing enough to kill him, after the game the boys from the other school seriously started looking for Cooper so they could beat him up, they were so jealous!

A crush can happen any time; even with someone you've known since kindergarten, but most commonly, you develop a crush on someone whom you just met or don't even know. Boys and girls will sometimes develop crushes on someone older than themselves, such as a teacher or the friend of a parent. You can even experience a crush, get past it, and then develop a crush again all over the same person.

## How To Handle A Crush

A crush can be one of the most emotional experiences of your life. How can you possibly survive it? Here are a few suggestions:

- First of all, remember that crushes are common and normal. They don't signal that you're losing your mind nor that your body is out of control. Rather, they are signs that you are growing up. Learn to recognize a crush when it happens to you, and thank God for the new feelings you are experiencing!

- Remember that you are a very attractive person just exactly the way God made you. Whether or not you are interested in a girl or boy or whether or not he or she is interested in you — neither affects the fact of how precious and beautiful you are to God!

- A crush will usually pass in a few weeks, no matter how intensely you're feeling in the beginning. The urge to see him or her will subside and you'll feel in more control of yourself. Once you've had a chance to get to know the person better, you may discover things you don't really find attractive after all, and your interest will naturally subside. On the other hand, you may discover that you still admire this person. Even as the emotional energy subsides, you are drawn toward him or her. You may have just survived the first stage of a really great relationship!

How the person you have a crush on responds to you can seem to make you or break you. If he or she enjoys your attention and sends back signals to keep it coming, you will probably feel happier than a teen in an electronics store. You might start singing when you walk, acting unusually kind toward your siblings, and even taking out the trash without complaining! Everything in your life may seem to brighten up.

If this person acts uninterested, or outright rejects you, the hurt can be overwhelming beyond words!

Todd continues his story:

I was fortunate that my first crush over Donna was a pretty positive experience, but my next crush was just the opposite. Megan was the cutest girl in my seventh grade class and she spoke with this wonderful French accent. In the beginning, we walked home from school together. Her flirting, her notes, her smiles captured my heart immediately, but Megan grew tired of me after a few weeks. She stopped meeting me after school, and when I asked her what was up she just told me to "flake off." I then found out she was going out with a new guy the next day. Oh, the pain I felt! I didn't come out of my room all weekend!

Instead of "having" a crush, Todd now "felt" crushed! The wonderful joy he experienced in the beginning was transformed into the awful pain of rejection and disappointment.

You, too, will sometimes experience rejection by someone you like. It's inevitable. When this happens, remember again that you are precious to God and nothing will change that! In fact, experiences like this can even help you to understand and treasure God's love more than ever. Find someone you trust whom you can talk to. Your mother or father will very likely understand. Believe me, they've experienced rejection, too. Be assured that the disappointment will pass. In a few days or weeks you won't feel the pain, and you may even find yourself interested in someone new!

## Moving Beyond a Crush

The ecstasy of a crush is usually based on fantasy, and has very little to do with reality, but imaginary as it is, a crush may be the first step in what will become a good, even wonderful, relationship between you and that special guy or girl. Relationships tend to go through predictable stages, like these:

• **Attraction**

This is where you first notice one another. Something about the person grabs your attention; their hair, dress, smile, athletic ability, or musical talent. You make up your mind this is someone you want to spend time with.

- **Exploration**

    In this phase you get to know one another. You walk between classes together, talk in the lunchroom, you speak by phone in the evenings, you may even meet together with a group of friends. "Flirting" is a great word to describe this playful phase of checking each other out.

- **"Dating"**

    If you both discover that you really like one another, you may move into a short-term commitment to "date" or "go out" with each other. "Dating" means different things at different ages. In the beginning, it may mean that you ask your best friend to ask his/her best friend if they think he/she likes you. Later on, it may mean you actually meet at the mall or go to a movie together. In any case, dating usually means that you promise to only go out with that person.

- **Crisis**

    Most teenagers only date one person for a few weeks at a time. One or both of them will then decide to move on. This "breaking up" can seem very hard, but it's also very normal, even healthy. Enjoying casual relationships like these can give you important experience you'll need for building relationships later on. They help you to develop confidence, communication skills, and to refine just what sort of person you are attracted to.

    As you develop experience with relationships, you'll learn to recognize which stage you are in at the moment, and you will be more prepared for what stage is coming up next.

# TRUE LOVE

Every young person wants to be loved, so it's only natural that we look for relationships where we can find them, but many relationships are actually built around popularity and prestige, not closeness or true friendship. The intention is really conquest or image, not affection or warmth. At the core, some people's motives are entirely selfish, just the opposite of the healthy love that we all need. So we must learn to tell the difference between love and selfishness. It starts with understanding about the three distinct types of love:

• **Friendship love**

This is attraction that occurs between companions or playmates. Adults sometimes call this by its Greek language name: *phileo* love. You've probably already experienced this kind of love between yourself and neighborhood friends. You've ridden bikes together, played with dolls or Legos or computer games, hiked in the woods, and shared lots of stories between yourselves. Through these experiences, you've developed a bond and trust in each other, one that may last for years or even a lifetime.

• **Romantic love**

Adolescence is the time when people first begin to feel incredible magnetism to the opposite sex. It's this physical attraction that sets romantic love apart from all the rest. Sometimes this is called erotic love, or simply "eros."

A distinctive trait about romantic love is that the feelings come and go over time. One week you may feel extremely drawn to a guy or girl. The next week those feelings are almost gone, only to return with new intensity the following week. Romantic love is what's at the heart of crushes. It's also the reason that crushes tend to quickly wear off, and that young couples change partners regularly. Romantic love feeds on the strong, exciting feelings that accompany it. Once these feelings begin to subside, relationships that are centered around romantic love alone usually unravel very rapidly.

## A Word of Caution: Guard Your Heart!

"Hearts" are perhaps the most fragile creation in all the universe. Hearts are easily broken and not so easily mended. Adolescents who rush into emotional relationships often leave high school with big, painful scars across their hearts. A boy or girl who is not careful often "falls in love" a dozen or more times before getting married. As fun as it seems to let these romantic feelings run wild, remember that somebody's almost always going to get hurt. There are few injuries in life that sting as badly as a broken relationship with the opposite sex during adolescence, especially when one of you has fallen way too hard, way too fast.

You can control your emotions, even the romantic kind, just like a marathon runner paces his speed for a long race. If the distance runner sprints the first 200 meters of the race, he'll probably collapse after the first mile. Likewise, guard your heart. Don't give away your love too quickly. First, get to know one another and discover whether this person is really worth the emotional investment. In the long run of life, you'll be glad you waited for just the right one!

**Nicholas Comninellis & Joe White**

• **Commitment love**

This is the strong, enduring kind of love that motivates people to give up things that are important to them so they can help someone else. It stays alive even when it hurts. You've probably seen this kind of love expressed by your parents toward you and toward other people. In Greek, this is known as *agape* love.

I remember going grocery shopping with my parents when I (Nicholas) was about eight years old. It was a Friday afternoon, the time when we usually stocked up for our trip to the lake that evening, but unlike normal shopping trips, my parents were purchasing very unusual items: towels, silverware, bed sheets, lots of canned goods, and even a toaster. I protested, "But Dad, we've already got this stuff! We don't need to buy any more!" Dad just smiled and commented, "You'll see, son."

From the store, instead of driving to the lake, we drove directly to the town dump located on the edge of the Missouri River. Now I really felt bewildered! Dad pulled the car to a stop in front of a burned-out trailer home. It still smelt of fresh soot, and whips of smoke rose from where the bedroom used to be.

From a tent pitched next to the trailer emerged an elderly couple, looking exhausted and anxious. I recognized them. They were the people who ran the dump! I remembered the story, too, that my dad told me just that morning. These were the ruins of the couple's home where my dad, a volunteer firefighter, had battled a blaze just the night before.

Mom and Dad opened the car trunk and started unloading our gifts of food and other essentials. With tears in their eyes, the surprised couple eagerly received our gifts. The greatest gift was the one I received: a real life demonstration of commitment love.

 **WHAT DO YOU THINK?**

- What were your emotions like the first time(s) you felt interested in someone of the opposite sex?

- What kind of advice would you give to a friend who is feeling a crush for someone?

- How have you or would you deal with your feelings after being rejected?

- What do you suppose is the best way to let someone know you are not interested in him or her?

- How is a crush different from true love or commitment love?

- What example can you give of true love in action?

 **FOR TEEN EYES ONLY**

To make romantic love, or even friendship love, last any length of time requires the addition of commitment love. Romantic love is mostly centered around getting affection from another person — and that can become selfish very quickly. Friendship love also depends upon receiving attention and respect from one another. It will die otherwise, but commitment love is all about giving, helping, understanding, and supporting another person, even if you don't receive much in return. Add commitment love to friendship or romantic love and you'll have the ingredients for some pretty wonderful relationships. Leave out the commitment, and you'll find that relationships die and you are alone much more than you'd like.

The Bible gives a terrific description of true love: It can be paraphrased like this:

> People with love in their hearts are patient and kind toward others, never acting jealous, boastful, or arrogantly. They don't behave poorly or selfishly, and don't hold grudges. People who truly love never wish evil upon anyone, but instead always work for the well being of others (1 Corinthians 13:4–7).

True love is not simply a strong emotion. Rather, it's a decision to give your attention, assistance, and affection to another — even if it sometimes hurts. In this sense, there is no real "love at first sight." Certainly there is attraction or infatuation at first sight, but true love, commitment love, is one that can only be developed and proven over time through real relationships.

Be very careful to not confuse true love and sexual desire. They are completely different. Many people do not understand this, however, leading to a very common, very tragic type of situation. Many girls have sex with guys as a way to fill their desire for love and admiration — thinking that the guys really feel the same way about them, but all the while the guys are saying they love the girls, not because they really do, but because it's a door opener to get what they really want — sex alone.

James Dobson, president of Focus on the Family, identified the problem exactly when he observed, "Boys experience a more persistent want for sex, whereas girls face a more emotional desire for closeness and intimacy."[1]

Learn to tell the difference between real love and sexual attraction. If you confuse the two, you'll likely discover that you have been horribly used by a boyfriend or girlfriend whom you thought really loved you, or that you've abused someone who believed that you really cared.

**Notes**

1. James Dobson, *Preparing for Adolescence* (Ventura, CA: Regal Books, 1979), p. 103.

"It happens when **two people wait** for just the right person,"

**9** **Nine Things**
**Countdown to Adolescence**

**Chapter**

**3**

# Sex . . . Waiting for the Best

## GETTING TO THE CORE

You may have already experienced feelings of physical attraction or romantic love. If not, it probably won't be much longer until you do. These kinds of feelings are the beginning of what eventually draws two people to have sex together. It's important to know what the attraction is like and how to handle it.

When a couple feels strong physical attraction for each other, they usually want to be closer and closer together: to cuddle, to kiss, to caress each others bodies — even to undress one another, and to have sexual intercourse.

Sexual attraction is an extremely powerful force, one that can result in incredible happiness and good. It can make you feel more warm and wonderful than you've ever imagined. It can help create incredible closeness between you and your mate. Sex can also lead to the birth of your child and the start of your own family.

However, sex can also lead to excruciating heartache and pain. Your parents can undoubtedly share with you stories about people who experienced the tragic consequences of sex. Why is sex so risky? Because there are some very big issues at stake, including your self-respect, your physical health, and the possibility you'll create a new baby. Your sexual behavior can also have a big impact on your relationship with God. How you decide to handle your sexual desires will dictate whether sex is a source of happiness for you, or a source of agony.

Let's first talk about the very best sex. It happens when two people wait for just the right person, then develop a very strong love, and finally commit themselves to spending their lives together. A terrific marriage relationship creates the perfect atmosphere in which the two can enjoy sex to the fullest.

Sex between two who are married is completely honorable, so no one's reputation is at stake. Since the couple commit to only have sex with one another, it's very unlikely they'll transmit any diseases to each other (more about this in a moment). If the woman becomes pregnant, the couple has a strong relationship in which to raise a child, and since God expects us to save sex for marriage, our obedience honors Him.

You've undoubtedly heard people on TV or in the movies slam sex in marriage as being boring or dull. Actually, the case can be just the opposite. Saving sex exclusively for the love of your life is far superior to any other alternative. Why? Because it is rooted in the security of a relationship built on affection, devotion, and commitment.

To eventually enjoy this kind of sex you must appreciate that sex is more than just a physical act. Sex starts with a desire in your head and in your heart, so learning to control sexual urges and thoughts is essential if you're not going to constantly struggle with the temptation of sex. TV, movies, websites, and your friends will begin to bombard you with messages saying that you should be having sex while you're a teenager. Now is the time to prepare for this onslaught. Decide to keep your mind from dwelling on thoughts of sex. Your friends may be looking at pornography or actually having sex with their partners. They may taunt you for not doing the same, but don't let them pressure you.

Having sex with your wife or husband is something that is years off in the future, but for the very best sex, it is worth the wait. In the meantime, go ahead and develop friendships with boyfriends or girlfriends. Enjoy each other's company, respect each other, and learn how to build one another up. Don't derail your teenage years or these healthy friendships with the lure of premature sex. This is exactly Robby's objective:

> My sister got married two weeks ago, and I saw the most beautiful and happiest marriage in my entire life. My sister is very close to God, and in her dating relationships in college and in high school she put God first. Last year, she met the neatest Christian man, one who has the same morals she does about Christianity. You had to be there to see the joy on their faces because

for their whole lives they saved the purity of their bodies for that day. I want that joy on my wedding day, too. I want to look my wife in the face on that day and say, "I love you and God so much that I saved my sexual purity for when it was meant to be, which is now." I look up to my sister for her strength and her love for God. I pray that some day I can have the same joy she had two weeks ago.

John and Mary got to enjoy that incredible ecstasy, thanks in part to Mark's faith and convictions. It all began when Mark started dating a young lady named Mary. He had made a commitment in advance to never go beyond kissing. At night when he'd come home from his dates with Mary, Mark's roommate, John, would question him about the physical side of the relationship. Mark would always tell John the same story. "John, we only kiss. That's the way it's going to be. I want her honeymoon and marriage to be pure and guilt-free, whether it's me she eventually marries or someone else."

John would even poke fun at Mark for his convictions in a way that only college roommates can do, but Mark held his ground.

As the months went by, Mark and Mary decided to break up and remain "just friends" for a lifetime.

Guess who began dating Mary after that?

You guessed it . . . John.

They dated, fell in love, and were married.

Guess who was John's best man?

You guessed it again . . . Mark.

After a wonderful wedding, John put his arm around Mark and with tears of gratitude in his eyes said to his best friend, "Mark, I used to kid you about being so pure with Mary. But, buddy, I can never thank you enough for treating her like you did. I owe you more than you'll ever know."

## THE WORST SEX

Sex can be wonderful, but having sex is also potentially very risky. If you give in to the pressure to have sex, you lay yourself open to incredible kinds of pain. To name a few:

### • Shame

We all want to be respected by our friends and peers. Building and protecting our reputation is one of the reasons we work hard at sports and music, try to keep our grades up, and be faithful to our friends.

Sex outside of marriage has just the opposite effect. Once you start "doing it," the word will get out. Your reputation will inevitably go downhill, and people won't look up to you like before. Ultimately, men do not respect women who are sexually active, and tend to quickly become bored with them. Likewise, women do not respect men who only have sex on their minds and are not so likely to go out with them.

Unfortunately, this sex-induced shame is a subject never highlighted in the movies, seldom addressed by parents, and even more rarely touched upon in school "sex education" classes. A good reputation is a great goal, but it comes at a price. If you become sexually involved, there is nothing that will protect your reputation.

By the time I (Nicholas) was a junior in high school, I already had a solid reputation as a leader in band, cross-country, and student council, but in one evening I almost lost everything I'd built. My girlfriend Erin and I were out walking around her neighborhood. It was a warm, dark night. After a while we stopped and sat down in a vacant lot. Erin and I were just talking and laughing when a car drove up and stopped. Out poured a group of guys from school.

"Hey, we know what you two were doing out there!" they jeered. "Makin' love in the tall grass. Wait 'til we spread the news! Ha! You were having sex! Your name is going rock bottom downward!" The sneering fellows hopped back into their car and sped away.

Sure enough, Monday morning I had some explaining to do. Though Erin and I were never sexually involved, we made the mistake of giving people an excuse to believe we actually were. Even that small "hit" on my reputation took months to recover from.

Here's a timeless fact: Premarital sex and a good reputation are completely incompatible. They never, ever fit together.

• Disease

Sex involves exchange of body fluids. When two people have sexual intercourse, a white colored fluid called semen (containing sperm) is ejected from the man's penis into the woman's vagina. There is also lubricating fluid in the woman's vagina that can enter back into the man's penis.

Several infections can be spread from the man to the woman and the woman to the man by way of these fluids. These are called "venereal diseases" or "sexually transmitted diseases." They are very common, and you've heard about some of them before. They go by names such as GC, gonorrhea, chlamydia, clap, syphilis, and herpes. HIV, which ultimately causes AIDS, is also transmitted from one person to another via sexual intercourse. These diseases can cause fever, pain, bleeding, infertility (the inability to become pregnant), cancer, and even death.

Modern medicine has treatments for these diseases, but no treatment is 100% successful. In fact, a cure for some sexually transmitted diseases — such as HIV — has yet to be found, and may never be found.

Here's a fact that is rarely mentioned: The only way to totally protect yourself from getting a disease through sex is to not have sex at all, plain and simple.

Some people will say that a condom will protect you, that it will allow you to have "safe sex." A condom, sometimes called a "rubber," is like a thin rubber glove that fits over the end of the penis. It helps to keep the man's sperm from contacting the woman's vagina during intercourse. It also helps to keep the woman's vaginal fluids from entering the man's penis.

The truth is that condoms do not provide complete protection. Some condoms make it to the store shelves even though they have holes in them from faulty manufacturing. Condoms must also be put on properly to work right, and people frequently put them on the wrong way. Even when put on correctly, condoms sometimes break while in use.

Here's another clincher that they never tell you in health class or sex ed. Condoms provide absolutely zero protection for:

- A boy or girl's virginity
- A girl's reputation
- A boy's memory of sexual experiences
- A couple's purity and development of friendship
- Protecting a girl or boy's respect for one another
- Protecting a girl or boy's delicate self-image

One Sunday morning I (Nicholas) was on duty in the emergency department of a small-town hospital. A 15-year-old girl came in with great tears rolling down both cheeks. She described excruciating pain when she urinated, and also of rawness around her vagina. These symptoms pointed toward the diagnosis of a typical bladder infection, but just to make sure, I examined her completely.

What I discovered was the worst case of herpes I'd ever seen in my career. The poor girl's entire vagina and labia, the skin surrounding the vaginal opening, were covered and encased by red blisters, causing her skin to tear and bleed with each movement of her legs.

As I explained how she got the infection, the young lady erupted into wailing, but this time it was not over the pain. Hers was a wail of deception discovered:

Everyone told me that sex was safe, as long as my boyfriend used a rubber! It was supposed to protect me from everything, but it didn't! I've been betrayed!

I prescribed her medication to fight off the infection, and to combat the pain. A short time after she left the ER a young man came in the door. Guess what? He was complaining of awful pain and sores on his penis. Examining him, I discovered just what I suspected: a horrible case of herpes.

As I talked with him about the infection, the young man became livid.

But that's impossible! Condoms are supposed to make sex "safe"! I've been swollen for days, but just knew it couldn't be a sexual infection. Then I got this call from my girlfriend. Now we both realize we've been totally lied to about safe sex!

I resonate with the anger experienced by these two young people. The information spread about condoms somehow making sex risk-free is simply false. If you want to truly protect yourself against all these diseases you must say no to sex.

• Pregnancy

It is remarkably easy for a girl to become pregnant. All it takes is sexual intercourse just one time. It can even happen the very first time a couple has sex together, and what was supposed to be a "fun" sexual encounter can suddenly lead to enormous guilt, broken dreams, and a drastic change in plans. Robbin experienced them all:

When I met Bobby I trusted him to know how far we could go without making love. He was in the driver's seat. He was also insecure. He would tell me over and over how he loved me, how he was sure that I didn't love him as much as he loved me. It was then that I set out to prove it. I was his —110% his. The first time we made love, I had no idea what was going on. Afterward, he didn't speak, he passed out. I was so alone. I've never hated myself more, but it was done. My virginity was gone.

It didn't matter after that. Sex became an

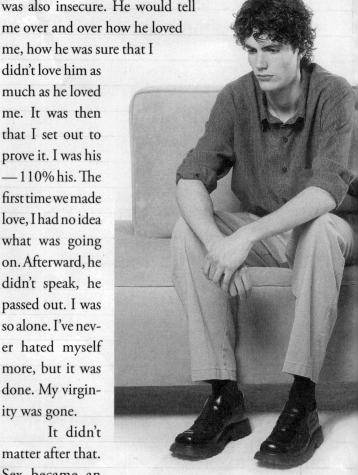

every day occurrence. My only fear was losing Bobby. He was the first, and even if he treated me bad (and there were those times), I was going to do anything I could to hang on to him, but slowly we drifted apart. He wanted to go out with other girls. I loved him, and he fooled me into thinking he loved me too. The day I left for the summer we made love. Yeah, it was fun — but it was just actions. That same evening, he told me he was going to see other girls.

I went through misery the next ten days being away, 'cause I discovered I was carrying Bobby's baby. How was I going to explain this to Bobby? Then I began to scheme. I got excited and thought, *Sure, he'll want to get married.* Finally, I had him, and if not him, I had a part of him anyway. I wouldn't have an abortion. That was out of the question. I'd either marry Bobby or run off and have the child myself.

Funny how Bobby controlled

my mind. I told him one night after we had made love down in his basement. I thought since he was so in love with me, that now was the time to break the news. He really lost it — he got all defensive and said that there was no possible way he could marry me and that he didn't even want to. I got scared and told him I was just kidding. He breathed a sigh of relief, but remained cold. It was not too long after that I told him the truth and had the pregnancy confirmed by a doctor. Bobby stuck by his guns about not marrying me and said if I kept the child, we were through.

At that point, I was helpless. I wanted more than anything to talk to my mom, but I could not hurt her with this kind of news. Looking back now, I should have talked to her. Bobby stuck by me long enough to make sure I had the abortion. He called me every day or wrote and made me feel like he still cared. I went in one day by myself to do the one thing I was most against. I talked to Bobby that night, and then he took off. He stuck around long enough to make sure I got rid of the evidence, then left me on my own.

I can't explain the feelings I have inside me now. I've never thought less of myself or felt more like trash. How could I have been so naive? I loved him, but he never knew the meaning of the word. I still have nightmares and at times I hate myself. Abortion is much, much deeper than the scraping of that uterus lining. It destroyed my baby and my self-respect. I'm left with only a guilt-ridden existence.

Why is pregnancy one of the most tragic consequences of sex outside of marriage? For the girl, education and career plans suddenly must take second seat to caring for a new baby. The boy usually refuses to accept responsibility for the new life and ends his relationship with the girl. The parents must also become involved. There may be pressure for the couple to marry long before they are grown up enough to handle such a relationship. Lawyers and courts also enter the picture to make rulings about who is responsible for the baby and who must pay the bills.

Caring for a baby and raising a child is extremely demanding, even in the most ideal situation, but bring a baby into a world of teenage parents with little experience, time, money, education, or social support, and the equation often spells disaster.

What about alternatives? Abortion — killing the innocent unborn baby — is out of the question. Letting the baby be adopted by a mature couple who are ready to be parents is often the best option in such situations.

By far the best alternative is simply to never get pregnant in the first place. As in the case of preventing sexually transmitted diseases, there are those who tout the use of condoms as a way to prevent pregnancy, but there is no condom that is 100% effective. The only way to be sure you won't get pregnant if you're a girl, or to be certain you won't become a father if you're a guy, is to not have sex.

**Nicholas Comninellis & Joe White**

This was Sam's decision:

> Honestly, tragedy is one of the main reasons why I never got sexually involved before marriage. I saw what a wreck pregnancy caused in the lives of my friends. Sure, I was hotly tempted. I had numerous girls offer to sleep with me, but with God's help I managed to stand my ground. Then, when I was 18, I witnessed an event that galvanized my decision for good: the birth of a baby. Amazing! To appreciate that this is what sex could lead to was even more incentive to hold out until I was married.

• **Guilt**

God knows all about these hazards. That's why He instructed us to save sexual intercourse for marriage alone. God's not trying to take the fun out of sex. On the contrary, He's trying to maximize the terrific pleasure we can have when we save sex exclusively for our one true love. What's more, God is trying to protect us from the incredibly harmful consequences that can happen if we become sexually active in any other relationship. Rob learned about this the hard way:

> I had been dating this girl for about five or six months. She was my first real girlfriend. After a few months, I started testing her to see how far she would let me go. She kept letting me do whatever I wanted. Well, I believe we went too far. We

never had sex, but it got to the point where all we would do on dates would be snuggle and touch each other.

I knew it was wrong, and I started feeling very guilty about all that was taking place. We were best friends, and now we were only talking every once in a while. It took a year before I asked God to forgive me for what I had done. During that year, I had many nightmares about how I had abused this girl and I felt so guilty. I still have bad memories of the experience, and I know that the devil keeps bringing it up, but I also know now that God forgave me for what I did.

Think about it. God is the one who thought up sex in the first place. He's the one who designed our amazing bodies, equipped our minds, and described the secrets for healthy relationships with others. God is by far the most reliable person to show us how to have wonderful lives — including how to enjoy sex to the fullest.

When we go ahead and get sexually involved with someone, we not only risk shame, disease, and pregnancy, we also put our relationship with God at risk. We distance ourselves from our wisest Counselor and greatest Friend. Ignoring God's instructions is like deciding to go live alone in the desert. The farther we move into the wasteland, the more we cut ourselves off from the shelter, food, and water we need to survive.

Sex outside of marriage is not the only thing that is wrong. So are lustful thoughts, fantasies about sex without actually doing anything. Why are fantasies such a big deal? Because dwelling on these dreams is the first step toward actually acting on them.

Virtually all teenagers struggle over sexual temptation. Maybe you've already been lured by sexual thoughts or pornography. Maybe you've even had sex, but regardless of whatever sexual experience lies in your past, there is great news: God will forgive you if you just ask.

A "virgin" is a person who has never had sex before. Virginity is a wonderful quality, one worth protecting all the way until your wedding night. The truth is that you can go back to not having sex even if you've already crossed that line in the past. We call this "renewed virginity." No matter how sexually active you have been — either physically or only in your mind — you can turn around and enjoy the virtue of being a virgin again. You can hold out for the very best sex in the future.

## WHAT DO YOU THINK?

- Why is it a good idea to save your deepest affection for your future husband or wife?
- Why do you think God wants you to save sex for when you are married?
- What do people risk when they start having sex before they are married?
- If you have been sexually active in the past, what can you do about it now?
- How can you prepare for sexual temptation before it ever happens?

Sexual attraction is all part of God's wonderful plan for our lives. It's only dirty or disgusting or terrifying when we abuse this God-given desire. Some day you will be tempted — extremely tempted — to have sex with someone. You'll be alone with a good-looking individual who will let you know they want sex with you. In the heat of the moment, you'll have a hard time keeping a clear head. The very best way to prepare for this encounter is to decide in advance how you will respond. Then when the moment arrives you'll be ready to stand up and say no.

Michelle was sweet 16 and had never been kissed (although her attractive features left many boys who wanted to be the first standing in a long line). She came to me (Joe) one day quite concerned because she "had never liked a boy, never wanted to kiss anyone, and sex would never be an issue with her." I assured Michelle that she was perfectly normal in every way and indeed some day the right boy would come along and she would have a passion that only God could control.

Within a matter of months, the school heartthrob, a guy named Rick, came into Michelle's life. He not only gave her her first kiss but wanted more . . . much more. Michelle discovered her affection for boys on that first date, but because of her abiding faith in God and her desire for purity, she let Rick know that kissing was absolutely her limit. It wasn't long before Rick moved on to easier territory, and Michelle was proud she said no.

**Nicholas Comninellis & Joe White**

The very best sex is the sex that two people reserve for the "one true love" of their lives. If you don't learn to control this desire now you will later dearly wish that you had.

More and more young people are realizing this fact, and deciding to reserve sex only for when they are married. Friends may taunt you that this is "old fashioned," but, unlike them, you won't be concerned about shame, disease, or pregnancy. You may even find yourself feeling closer to God, and someday, when the time is right and the relationship is real, genuine love, you'll be ready to enjoy the sex that's absolutely worth the wait!

"When you call someone a **real friend,** you are saying, **'I love you.'** "

**9** **Nine Things**
Countdown to Adolescence

# Chapter 4

# Finding Real Friends

## GETTING TO THE CORE

As a child, you spent most of your time interacting with your parents, brothers, and sisters. As you got a little older, you began to play with neighbors and the other kids in grade school. Friends were often fun to hang out with, but almost always secondary in importance to your family.

As you approach the teenage years, friends take on a new priority. You discover that you want more than just the security and familiarity of those at home. You want real friends of your very own, the kind of deep, lasting, encouraging relationships you've heard about and seen other people enjoy.

"Enjoy" is a key word. Ideally, friends help us learn about ourselves. They help us create our own individuality, but most of all, friends are a key to happiness in life. Without them, people are often left feeling lonely, incomplete, and out of place.

This transition from family to friends is, all in all, a healthy one. It marks your growing independence from your parents and siblings, and is another step toward becoming a fully developed, independent person.

## TRUE FRIENDS

One of the biggest challenges for teenagers is learning to recognize and attract *genuine friends*. Just as some "love" is actually selfishness in disguise, some "friendship" is also deceptive. We've had the privilege of talking to thousands of teenagers and university students about friendship and happiness. We've asked several hundred to write down what real friendship means to them. We'll quote a few of their responses that best convey what almost all of them are saying:

- "A friend is someone who is truly loyal to you and wouldn't do anything to hurt the other mentally or physically" (Bill, age 15).

- "A friend is someone who will always stick by you and never makes you do things you don't want to. He is loving and caring and will always have something kind and encouraging to say" (Jason, 14).

- "The kind of friend that I would like to have would be someone who always encourages me, who is always my friend no matter what happens to me. A friend is honest and isn't snobby" (Alice, 16).

- "A friend is someone I can trust, someone who can make me laugh, someone who will like me as I am, someone I can have fun with, and someone who will try to make me better" (Paula, 14).

- "A friend is someone who will listen to my thoughts and try to help me with my problems. They don't make fun of me. It is someone I can trust" (Julie, 15).

- "A friend is a person who is never rude and does not lie and helps me when I'm sad and never talks behind my back and always sticks up for me and doesn't pressure me" (Barb, 14).

- "Someone I can trust — someone I can be with always — someone I can love forever" (Randy, 16).

- "A friend is a person I can get along with; I can share something with them without fear of it being told. Someone who lifts me up when I'm down" (Susan, 13).

- "A friend is someone who during hard times can put a smile on my face and make everything seem better, yet a friend is also someone who will celebrate my victories with me without jealousy" (Ginger, 16).

- "A true friend is one who will not try to lead me into sin. He is also one whom I can trust and have fellowship with. This friend accepts me as I am, and he never tries to change me" (Sam, 16).

- "A friend is someone who cares about me and likes me as I am; someone who doesn't pressure me into doing things I don't want to do; someone I can trust and be able to tell things to" (Peter, 14).

You get the picture. True friendship means unselfishly looking out for the good of one another. You can tell a true friend by the way he or she responds to your own needs. A true friend is someone who sincerely asks how you are, does not gossip about you, is patient towards you, and who calls or e-mails just to check up on you. Once you find a friend like this, you'll probably want to hang on to him or her! When you call someone your friend, you are giving that person about the highest compliment you could possibly give. You're saying, "You really make me happy," but even more than this, you're also saying, "You can trust me. Don't be afraid because I'll never intentionally let you down."

Finally, when you call someone a real friend, you're saying, "I love you" — because real friendship is all about love. It's both the "phileo love" and the "commitment love" we talked about in chapter two. This kind of relationship is one of the most pure, exhilarating experiences you can ever enjoy in life.

## False Friends

While your parents almost always have your best interests at heart, the same cannot always be said of your peers. They may criticize you for no good reason, use demeaning nicknames, avoid picking you for sports teams, leave you out of conversations, not invite you to parties, and a thousand other things to make you feel low.

At times, these peers will demand that you behave in ways you would never think of. They may tempt you to go against your parents, to slack off in school, start using drugs or alcohol, become sexually involved, or even to commit crimes. Yet out of desire to be accepted by the group — any group — young people sometimes do what they know is going to get them in trouble.

Listen to Trent's story:

> When I was starting high school I knew
> only a few people. I longed to get in with a group

of friends, so I began hanging out with some cool guys who sat in the back of my math class. We'd often play a little basketball together after school, and then go for pizza. I began to really like these guys, and to hope they'd keep letting me into their group.

One weekend I got what appeared to be a big break. They were having a party, and invited me over. Oddly, they asked me to bring along a blowtorch from my dad's shop. What's more, it didn't turn out to be the music, chips, video, and dancing kind of party I expected. Instead, I arrived to find the guys huddled in a basement cutting pipes.

"What are you up to?" I asked with interest.

They continued to work intently. "Look, are you here to help, or to just ask questions? Just shut up," said one. "Hey, where's your blowtorch? Okay, hand me that can of gunpowder," another demanded.

I felt bewildered as I observed their flurry of activity. "Trent, hold your finger here while I thread in the fuse," commanded one of the guys.

Suddenly it all made sense to me. My new "friends" were making pipe bombs — explosives that could instantly level an entire house! Whatever interest I had in making new friends suddenly evaporated. All I could think of was getting out of there before the police found out. I made up some excuse to go upstairs, then bolted out the front door, blowtorch in hand, and never looked back. I finally realized that these guys only wanted me for the tools they needed. Nothing more.

False friends will use you. They will also abuse you. Although I (Joe) had no idea at the time how damaging it was, my fourth grade friend Jerry did me the worst favor of my life when he brought photos of nude women over to my house that he had torn from his warped-minded father's secret magazines. The photos seemed fun to look at, much to my friend's delight, but the images caused me to continue to have lustful thoughts for years to come!

In truth, friends who introduce you to pornography, crime, drugs, alcohol, sex, and immoral music are worse than no friends as all. False friends will just try to take advantage of you — your attention, your popularity, your possessions, your money — in order to get something they want. You can detect false friends right away, especially if they:

- Gossip about you behind your back
- Lie to you to your face
- Steal your property
- Push you to take any kind of drugs
- Pressure you to look at pornography
- Urge you to do things that are illegal or dangerous

These "friends" may actually think they have good intentions toward you. They may sound sweet and sincere, even wise, when talking with you, but don't be fooled. First check out what they really want out of your friendship.

## GAY AGENDA

Some of the most sly and treacherous false friends are those who come on as genuine, but in reality simply want sex, but not the normal kind of sex between a man and a woman. These guys are looking to have sex with other guys. These girls are looking for sex with other girls. Sound strange? In some communities, homosexuality is unusual, but the trend is growing nationwide. Sound perverted? Absolutely! The gross character of men having sex with men, or women with women is completely nauseating, but everyone needs to know what it's about. Not only is homosexuality perverse beyond words, but many homosexuals are proud of their behavior and are looking to draw other young people into their web of perversion. Check out this confession of a former homosexual:

Gay is not good, nor is it a happy way to live. The very people who claimed they were happy where they were at, on a deeper level of communication, admitted they were miserable and had the lowest self-esteem later on. These people who claimed they were happy being gay were actually more miserable than the people who said they were miserable being gay! I talked to well over 200 individuals, and there were *no* exceptions to this. I myself fit into both categories at one time or another. Any homosexual — even if he doesn't admit it to anyone but himself — wishes that he were something other than what he has let himself become.

So test out your new friends before you become too involved with them. When you discover a person with a gay agenda, remember that no friendship is worth the trap they are setting for you.

## TIED TO THE PEER

Why do people seem to give in so easily to pressure from others? It starts from a healthy need for friends, but accompanying this need is also a strong pressure to conform to friends, to behave just like them. The pressure to conform is so strong that some people feel uncomfortable doing almost anything that differs from the group, whether it's the way they dress, the language they use, the music they listen to, or the sports or games they play. The pressure to conform also molds the attitudes teens adopt toward their parents, schoolwork, and even God.

Advertisers realize the importance of peer pressure, and take advantage of this fact to try and sell us products that we don't really need, but that "everybody else" has. Event promoters encourage us not be left out, because "all the people" will be there. Friends urge us to get involved with their particular sports or hobbies because, "We're all doing it!"

Not all conformity is bad. Sometimes group pressure actually helps protect us from hazards. Kids, for example, often ask their friends to ride their bikes to school as a group rather than to ride alone. More often, however, conformity to the group robs us of our individuality. It keeps us from developing our unique strengths and talents. The pressure to conform can even push us to make a fool of ourselves. Listen to Brad's story:

One vacation, I learned just how closely I was tied to the influence of my peers. Seven of my best friends came to spend the weekend on my family's boat at the lake. On the drive down, I was bragging about how well I could handle the boat, but when we all arrived at the dock, and my friends saw it, they questioned, "Hey Brad, can you really drive this thing?" I felt pretty pumped when my dad reassured, "Sure he can! Brad, show them how it's done!"

We got on board. My friends, including a couple of girls whom I dearly wanted to impress, stood on the rear deck as I walked around the perimeter of the boat, untying the lines that connected us to the pier. I felt so anxious to make a good showing I tripped over the anchor mounted on the bow and almost fell into the water.

Everyone was staring at me with this uncertain look. I fired up the twin engines, engaged the propellers, and advanced the throttles. The engines revved, the water churned, but the boat did not move. So I gave it more power. Still, the craft would not budge. Out of the corner of my eye, I saw my friends shake their heads and heard them whisper to one another, "He doesn't really know what he's doing!" They were laughing at me.

Mortified, I anxiously looked around. What could the problem possibly be? Finally, I saw it. In my attempt to impress my "peers," I overlooked the one rope that was still holding the boat bound to the "pier." I was immobilized by them both!

Peer pressure is like that. It's powerful, and frequently intimidating. In fact, as hard as teens can be on one another, it is amazing that anyone survives adolescence with their own personal opinions. Hair that's too short or not styled just right can make an otherwise attractive student be ignored. A teen that is successful at tennis may be rejected for not playing a more aggressive sport like football. Someone gifted at the violin may never be appreciated by their friends who prefer punk, pop, rock, or rap.

The truth is, however, you do not have to be like your peers. You can discover your own interests, develop your own talents, and explore your own dreams.

In fact, this is exactly what you should do! You are a unique person, a one-of-a-kind individual. As you move from being a kid to being a teenager, you'll experience feelings and opportunities like no one else. From these, you'll develop a personality that is 100% yours alone.

Most parents and teachers realize how important it is for you to form your own character, within reasonable guidelines. The Bible, too, encourages healthy individual development, saying, "Do not be conformed to this world, but be transformed by the renewing of your mind, that you may prove what is the will of God; that which is good, excellent, and perfect" (Rom. 12:2). God does not want us to simply follow the whims of the people around us. Rather, He wants us to follow eternal truths — ones that will make our lives happy and fulfilled.

Decide now to always do what you know is right, no matter what other people say. Then, you'll be prepared when they tempt you to drink alcohol, race cars, shoplift, smoke, listen to dirty jokes, look at pornography, and a thousand other habits that will harm you.

Realize now that you are incredibly valuable to God, regardless of anyone else's opinion. Then, you'll be ready when people assault you with criticism, pester you, and make up false stories that aim to drive you downward.

Think for yourself. Hold to your convictions. Resist the pressure to conform. Do so, and you'll eventually discover many people who'll think the world of you for NOT conforming!

## WHAT DO YOU THINK?

- What do you enjoy most about having friends? Why are they important to you?

- How would you describe a true friend? Name someone who is a true friend to you.

- What gives away a false friend? What are the warning signs you can look out for?

- How can false friends make trouble for you?

- Why is it important to not give in to peer pressure? Can some peer pressure actually be good for you?

- What do you suppose is the key to making good friends?

## FOR TEEN EYES ONLY

Everybody wants to have friendships, especially the kinds that are lively and encouraging. So what's the secret to success? Of all the advice we could possibly share, the first and foremost is simply this: To have a friend you first must be a friend. This means taking a risk and getting to know someone else. It means showing respect, giving honest compliments, sharing your time and attention with another.

If that person responds by treating you the same way, then you may well have found a friendship worth pursuing. Healthy friendship is an exchange where both people are giving — maybe not always the same amount or at the same time — but are consistently sharing their lives with one another. Over time, if you find the exchange is one sided, you must try to repair the imbalance, or let that friendship go.

Once you find a healthy friendship — one where you both appreciate and encourage what's good about each other — then hang on tight. There will be times of doubt, times when you begin to believe you'd be better off cutting loose, but for a true friend, almost any pain is worth enduring.

**Nicholas Comninellis & Joe White**

I (Joe) coached football at Texas A & M University under Coach Ben Stallings, a captivating personality. When he speaks, people listen intensely. We were in his pickup one autumn day going to see a boy in the hospital. Coach pulled up to a stoplight and looked over at me with those big brown eyes, and said with seriousness, "I want to tell you a story — it's a good one, and it's true. You listening?"

"Yes, sir, I'm listening."

The light turned green. As we pulled through the intersection he began, and as he continued he would look at me every few seconds to impress a certain point. "I was going to speak at a banquet the other night," he said, "and I was sitting in the car with an older gentleman. Between us on the seat was a very old scrapbook that had been in this man's family for generations. As I flipped through the pages of it, I came across a very interesting letter."

Coach Stallings looked me in the eye and added, "It wasn't a copy of the letter — it was the real thing."

I squirmed in my seat.

"The letter was from a 19-year-old boy named Sam Davis. Here's what he wrote:

Dear Mom and Dad,

Tomorrow I will be hanged. It's nothing you've done but I've gotten into trouble here in the war and they're going to hang me.

Love, Sam

Coach Stallings continued, "I couldn't wait to find out more about this Sam Davis, so I went to the history books and found out that he was a young Confederate spy in the Civil War, assigned to go behind the Union Army's lines and gather information. On one such spy mission he ran into another 19-year-old from the Union Army and became committed friends."

Now Coach Stallings looked at me to see if I caught his emphasis on the last phrase. I had.

"Those two 19-year-old friends stayed together for several days. As Sam was leaving to go back to his army, the Union soldier gave him some outdated maps of Union troop movements and said, 'Sam, these maps are no longer accurate, but put them into your saddlebags and take them to your general. They'll think you did a good job over here and give you a promotion.'

"Sam was probably laughing to himself as he went away. But while he was trying to cross the front lines, he was apprehended by a Union guard, who went through his papers and found the maps. 'Where did you get the maps, son?' he demanded.

" 'I'm not going to tell you.'

" 'You'll tell us all right!' He had Sam locked up.

"After a few days passed, the gallows were set up for Sam's hanging. Guards came to his cell to get him, and they made him ride to the gallows on his coffin, which was secured on a horse-drawn wagon. In front of the gallows they stopped, and a Union general approached the frightened young teenager. 'What's your name, son?' he asked.

" 'Sam Davis, sir.'

" 'Do you see those gallows? They're for you.'

" 'Yes, sir.'

" 'If you'll tell me where you got the maps, I won't hang you.'

"Sam replied, 'I can't tell you.'

" 'What do you mean you can't tell me? Didn't you hear what I just offered you?'

"Sam paused, then answered, 'I got the maps from a friend, sir, and I'm not going to tell you who he is.'

"The general looked intently into the teenager's eyes. 'Look, son,' he said. 'You're 19 years old and have a long life ahead of you. I don't want to hang you. I just want to know where you got the maps. If you'll just tell me who gave them to you, I'll personally escort you back across the lines to safety. Where did you get the maps?'

"With the boldness of a much older warrior, Sam Davis looked into the general's face and said, 'Sir, I'd die a thousand deaths before I'd bring trouble on my friend, and I am disappointed you would ask me to do it.' "

Coach Stallings stopped the truck, leaned his head toward me, and said, "Now that's true friendship. 'I'd die a thousand deaths before I'd bring trouble on my friend.' Joe, that's true friendship."

I got the message. Sam paid the ultimate price to protect his friend. Hopefully, you will never have to give up your life for another the way Sam did, but short of sacrificing your life, there are thousands of ways and a multitude of opportunities to develop great friendships while you're a teenager, friendships that will last for years and bring incredible joy into your life.

So offer friendship to those around you. Learn to distinguish who your true friends really are, while standing up for your own opinions. Avoid those who just want to take advantage of you, and once you find a true friend, be loyal to the end.

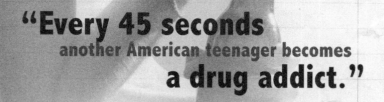

"**Every 45 seconds**
another American teenager becomes
**a drug addict.**"

**9** **Nine Things**
Countdown to Adolescence

# 5

# Public Enemy Number One

## GETTING TO THE CORE

Virtually all kids grow up knowing that alcohol and other drugs can hurt their relationships, harm their bodies, and even kill them. In fact, alcohol is the leading cause of death for young people in America. It's the public enemy that is behind so many car wrecks, suicides, assaults, murders, rapes, and drownings. It's the catalyst behind letters we have received like these:

JOEY — I care so much about people and what they do with their lives. I think it is such a tragedy to see so many teenagers today throw their lives away with drugs and alcohol. Just three days ago, two of my good friends were pretty badly injured in a drunk driving accident. They got in the car with two guys who had been drinking and they went into a guardrail on a bridge and went off. Needless to say, both of my friends were also drinking. The two guys weren't hurt, but my two friends got a broken jaw, ribs, and stitches.

SYBIL — One night, I decided to hang out with a good guy friend at his apartment. He was a freshman in college — I was a junior in high school. Going into the evening, I had no idea what was in store for me. I began the evening with a couple of drinks and a few shots. Very soon after that the alcohol had overcome some of my mind. Chris, my friend, and a few of his friends were smoking pot, something I had quit and promised myself I wouldn't do again, but I gave in to the pressure and soon was very high. The friends left and Chris and I started kissing. One thing led to another, and before I knew it, I was losing my virginity. Chris ignored my, "No, I'm not ready for this." Immediately, I passed out. I woke up to Chris forcing himself into me very strongly. The pain, regret, and hurt I have suffered could have all been prevented if only I had stayed away from the drugs.

MATTHEW — I've got to tell you about what really happened that night. It wasn't just rainy and slick like I told the police. We, my friends and I, had been drinking at a football game. We kept the booze inside our coats so no one would spot us. Well, after the game was over the five of us piled into my car. I was so drunk, I could hardly get my keys into the ignition. I tore out of the parking lot, onto the highway, flew over the hills, and landed right into a tree. We hit so hard it severed that two-foot trunk right in two, but that's not all it severed. Gabriel lost his leg. Bonnie lost an eye, and Mitch, poor Mitch, he lost everything. . . .

Alcohol abuse is rampant in our country. In a recent survey, 45% of fourth to sixth graders were drinking. High school kids around the country report that about three out of every four students they know drink. In college, that rate climbs to four out of five!

At this moment, there are four to five million full-blown teenage alcoholics in America. Many will never know total freedom from drugs ever again. Because of their addiction, tens of thousands of them in the future will suffer physical and financial ruin, face prison sentences, and inflict abuse on the very people whom they love.

Why? Virtually everyone is aware of the dangers of drinking, but they do it anyway. The number one reason is simple: peer pressure.

We often hear elementary kids say, "Drugs are gross! Why would anyone want to take that stuff?" But when kids enter adolescence, suddenly some of their friends start drinking, smoking, snorting, or injecting drugs. These same kids who used to comment that "drugs are gross," see their friends doing drugs and start to have second thoughts, along the lines of, "Maybe drinking and drugs are not so bad after all." Add more peer pressure to the picture, and these teens often start going down the drug road they swore they'd never, ever travel.

Almost all teenagers caught in this tragic trap were introduced to their first drink or drug by "a friend." Hundreds of letters we receive every year tell the same story: "My friend got me into this." It kills us to see what teenagers today will do in the name of friendship. Aren't true friends supposed to want the best for each other, to help one another succeed in life? Of course! That's why any "friend" who tries to push you toward alcohol or other drugs is actually no friend at all!

## FRIENDS YOU CAN ENJOY FOREVER

I (Joe) met a girl at Southern Methodist University during my senior year of college football. Each game, she stood cheering on the sidelines and always brought the crowd to their feet as she led our team into the stadium, doing round-off back handsprings down the astroturf. Debbie-Jo was probably the poorest girl at S.M.U. After losing her dad in a plane crash when she was four, her mom struggled with five kids just to keep the bills paid, but even though she didn't have the financial resources to shop at Neiman Marcus like many other S.M.U. girls did, Debbie-Jo came to class each day in the finest appearance you ever laid eyes on. Though she often wore only faded jeans and workout clothes, the "threads" I noticed on her were the fibers of her unquestionable reputation.

Reputation is how you really look. It's how you dress yourself every day . . . not in cotton or silk or nylon fabrics, but in the lifestyle that attracts men's or ladies' hearts (not just their eyes). I'll never forget calling Debbie-Jo at the Kappa Alpha Theta sorority house where she lived to interview her for a summer counselor position at our sports camp. Her roommate answered the phone and let me know that Debbie-Jo was at a party with the Sigma Alpha Epsilon fraternity.

I asked her roommate if Debbie-Jo would be drinking, and to my amazement, her roommate replied as if there wasn't ever a question, "Definitely not. Debbie-Jo never drinks."

Abstaining from alcohol said volumes about Debbie-Jo's character. No wonder the girls at S.M.U. respected her so. No wonder so many guys would have given anything to go out with her. No wonder I "fell over dead" for Debbie-Jo. No wonder Debbie-Jo, my wife today, continues to be more intimately attractive to me with each passing year!

Debbie Jo is not the only one saying no to alcohol. Our sports camps at Kanakuk have a staff of 2,500 collegiate Christian athletes. They're about the happiest, most attractive, fun, enthusiastic bunch of kid-loving people you'll ever possibly find. Though some have fallen during their teen years, all are now committed to holding out for sexual intimacy until they are married, and get this. None of the 2,500 drink the entire time they're working at Kanakuk. Most never drink at all, and won't throughout their entire lives.

Why? Because along with the health risks, they don't want to cause another person to stumble. They don't want to be that peer who influences, however minutely, another person to start drinking.

Do you really want to stay free from alcohol? Do you want to avoid the pain, embarrassment, and hopelessness of addiction? Then find friends like these; like Debbie Jo, like our Kanakuk staff. Surround yourself with friends who will help protect you from Public Enemy Number One.

## DREAMS GONE UP IN SMOKE

Imagine this: a 1,200 degree flame burning just one inch from your lips, gray-black ash and fumes swirling inside your nose, healthy pink cells dying by the millions within your chest, toxic waste flooding into your bloodstream.

This is what people do for fun?

Second only to alcohol, the other leading killer is tobacco. By the time they are 16 years old, three out of four teens have tried cigarettes, and half of them are addicted. What's more, teenage girls smoke more today than ever before!

Most people start their tobacco addiction during their teenage years. In fact, the chances are almost zero that a person will start smoking after they graduate from high school. The tobacco companies know this very well. That's why their ads are targeted toward you! Tobacco companies realize that if they can succeed in getting you hooked now, they've probably got you for life. Tobacco executives also acknowledge that if you resist them now, they will never capture you at all.

It's easy to identify people who smoke. The first sign is their unmistakable odor. If you get close enough, it's not hard to distinguish the smell of a smoker. Even if they have just brushed their teeth and washed their outfits, the scent of tobacco rarely comes out of their breath, hair, and clothing.

Tobacco also leaves telltale evidence on the teeth and fingers. It's a yellow, sometimes greenish stain. It can also accumulate on the lips and cheeks. Even one's chest and hands can get dingy with this discoloration. Simple scrubbing is rarely enough to get rid of the marks. Why?

**Nicholas Comninellis & Joe White**

Because the tobacco is not simply lying on top of the skin, it's actually absorbed within the body.

Even from a distance, smokers stand out. Their wrinkled skin is a dead giveaway! The wonderful, smooth, line-free face of a teenager is quickly seared by tobacco. What remains are "crows feet" — lines that extend from the corners of the eyes, furrows tracked across the forehead, and grooves that run down on either side of the nose. What's worse, the bright skin luster that characterizes youth is quickly replaced by a dull, pallid hue that only tobacco can generate.

As if this is not enough, all the while that tobacco is spoiling a young person's appearance, it is also wreaking havoc on the inside. To be able to competitively run, dodge, shoot, throw, and tackle, every system of the body must be in tip-top shape. Yet tobacco attacks virtually every system an athlete depends on.

The brain doesn't think as quickly. Lungs can't breathe as effectively. The heart beats with less power. Muscles contract with less precision. Eyesight becomes impaired. The entire athletic machine starts breaking down, just when a person needs to perform at maximum ability!

Consider this "tobacco revelation" reported by one student:

ANDRE — It all started innocently enough. I was at a friend's house after school a couple of years ago. We were sitting about playing some computer games, when he calmly pulls out a cigarette and lights up. I protested, "Won't your parents get upset?" "Oh, never," he replied. "They won't find out, 'cause I leave the windows open." Well, I didn't want to be left out, so when he offered me one, I lit up, too. I got kind of a rushing feeling, so I smoked another and another.

Wasn't long before I was completely hooked. I smoked before school, during lunch, while I was driving home. I smoked before practice, and right after drills. I began running low on money, so I got a grocery store job, but that just kept me out later at night, hanging out with my friends who also smoked.

This was no innocent habit. I began to lose the girls who liked me. "You smell like an ash tray!" one of them said as she gave me back my class ring. My parents sealed off my room, because it smelled so bad.

Then my coach took me aside one afternoon. "Andre," he started, "you're not playing so strong any more. I'm pretty certain it's that junk you've been inhaling. I'm putting you on the bench until things turn around."

I was crushed. I was infuriated. I was benched! All because I let a little burning stick get control of me!

Sadly, every day thousands of teenagers drop the convictions they held as kids and give into the pressure to smoke. Don't let yourself become a statistic. Don't repeat Andre's mistakes. Say no to Public Enemy Number Two.

## More Deadly Drugs

Tobacco and alcohol are not only deadly in themselves, they are also often the "door openers" into abuse of other, even more dangerous drugs: marijuana, cocaine, heroin, amphetamines, narcotics, and a host of others.

Every 45 seconds, another American teenager becomes a drug addict. As with alcoholism and tobacco use, the results are regularly tragic. We work with teenagers every summer who come to us begging for a way out of their addictions. Frequently with sorrowful expressions, wasting bodies, and tracks up and down their arms, they are a pitiful sight. Unable to keep a job, drug addicts are compelled to do anything for the next fix — prostitution, robbery, extortion — anything.

You see, it's not just the physical hazards of drugs. It's what they do to your entire life. It's how drugs break up the relationships that are most important to you. It's how they tempt you to get into sex. It's the way they destroy your performance in school, and wreck your success at sports. It's how they ruin your dreams for the future, and keep you shackled to drugs you absolutely hate but can't seem to ever break away from.

Kathy experienced how drugs lead her into a self-punishing lifestyle:

KATHY — I never thought I would regret sex so much. One night I was at a party and I got drunk and had sex with someone else while going out with my boyfriend. I felt awful, and I was scared of diseases. Then I made myself stop drinking because I knew if I wasn't drunk, I wouldn't have had sex. I didn't drink for a couple of months and felt a little better.

Then a friend introduced me to drugs. I promise this ties in with sex. When you start smoking pot, you begin to not care about anything else. I started seeing a guy friend who sold it. He wanted to have sex. I promised myself I wouldn't. Anyway, I did have sex with this awful guy and I became miserable — I'm still miserable. I've hurt everything about me. I can't even be happy unless I'm faking it, which is constant.

There are no "innocent" drugs. One drink, one puff, has become the first step straight downhill for millions of teens. Once you give in just a little, the door blows wide open to an onslaught of perils from other drugs. Don't ever let it happen. Keep your door locked tight.

## WHAT DO YOU THINK?

- What do some people find so attractive about drugs?
- What do drugs do to a person's ability to make good decisions? How do they affect one's will-power?

**Nicholas Comninellis & Joe White**

- What sorts of harm can come on a person when they can't think straight because of drugs?

- What do drugs do to a person's reputation at school? Is this a good thing?

- What role do friends play in getting a person addicted to drugs?

- Why is simply knowing about the temptation of drugs not enough? What else is required?

- Why is it important to decide how to respond to this temptation before it starts?

 **FOR TEEN EYES ONLY**

Teens are smart. They can spot trouble from miles away. Drugs are trouble, and every kid knows it's true.

Teens still get into drugs. Why? Because just being smart is not enough. You also have to take action. You have to keep distance between yourself and the people carrying drugs.

Almost all drug addition is the result of bad company. Once you adopt these kinds of "friends" and start hanging out with them, you've set yourself up for incredible temptations. You've all but guaranteed that you'll eventually cave in and do the things they do — even the stupid things like smoking, drinking, and doing other drugs.

On the other hand, you can decide to be both bright and brave. You can detect in advance those peers who will lead you into trouble. You can break your ties with them before they deceive and seduce you. You can instead find true friends who will help propel you toward the happiness and success you really want.

Dimitri was one young man who did just this. His sixth grade year lead him to a new school, filled with entirely unfamiliar students and demanding teachers. The adjustment was very hard on him. Dimitri felt frustrated, exhausted, lonely, and at times extremely angry. His parents were quite worried. They talked with their son at length, pored over his homework with him, got professional counseling, and prayed constantly.

Dimitri had been a pretty successful kid up to that point. He was into Boy Scouts, violin, and football, but as the year progressed, Dimitri began to lose interest in these. Instead, what Dimitri felt he needed most were friends, but the new school environment didn't seem to provide anyone promising.

Then one day Dimitri didn't come home from school until late. He told his parents he'd been at a new buddy's house. He pepped up as he described how awesome Kyle and Kevin were. Soon Dimitri was going to their house everyday. Instead of feeling happier, instead of having more energy for school, instead of feeling better about himself, Dimitri seemed to withdraw even more. His anger intensified. His grades plummeted. Something was terribly wrong.

School ended, and Dimitri went off to summer camp at Kanakuk. Returning two weeks later, his parents couldn't help but notice the difference. Their son had a glow about him, a confidence that was absent before. Dimitri became interested in school again. He took up violin lessons. He started spending time with a new friend he'd met at camp, and he never mentioned Kyle and Kevin again.

One afternoon, Dimitri's father found him in an unusually talkative mood.

"Tell me, son," his father coaxed, "what happened this summer that made you become so happy?"

"Well, Dad, you know those friends of mine, Kyle and Kevin. They were really, really bad. They were heavy into drugs, heavy into the occult. I wanted friends so bad, they almost got me to do stuff with them." Dimitri spoke with concern, and then switched to a tone of unusual confidence. "But while I was at camp this summer I told God I was not going to give in. I told Him I was going to cut loose from these guys, start living right, and find friends who'd help me follow God closer. And that's exactly what I did."

Dimitri's no more bright or brave than you, too, can be. Eventually, you'll hear the tempting voices, saying:

"Try it just this once."

"You'll know when to stop,"

"One beer won't hurt anybody."

"You can handle it."

"Real men do it, why don't you?"

Choose now how you're going to respond when you hear these invitations. In the heat of the moment, it may be too late. Choose now to be both bright and brave. When you look back, you'll see it's your own life you saved.

"...adolescence is a time when you're especially susceptible to new influences."

**9** **Nine Things**
Countdown to Adolescence

# Chapter

**6**

# Trash In/
# Trash Out

## GETTING TO THE CORE

When your parents were teens, they dealt with some of the same challenges you face: crazy emotions, feelings of love, the search for true friends, and the temptation of drugs, but there are new hazards on the scene; ones that did not threaten your parents nearly as much as they will threaten you. Their influence can infiltrate your mind, and eventually overtake your heart — all the while keeping you unaware of their incredibly powerful, often dangerous, impact.

We are talking about media — about the force of music, television, movies, computer games, and websites. Sure, music and video have been around for a long time, but not only is media more prominent today than ever before, now it's super-charged by computer-based, interactive programs.

Just how much exposure do teens have to media? The typical teenager spends 4 hours each day directly in front of some form of electronic "amusement," consuming almost whatever it serves up to them. Add listening to music to the mix, and the exposure goes up to 6 hours every single day. That's about 40 hours each week! Just how much is 40 hours? Well, it's as much time as most teens spend in school. It's the same number of hours most parents work during a week, and, it's almost as much time as kids spend talking on the phone!

By now you realize that adolescence is a time when you're especially susceptible to new influences. Advertisers know this fact very well. So do the media producers, which brings us to an important, sobering truth: Producers and advertisers will promote whatever they can possibly sell, period. The content of what they promote rarely matters. Whether the song, program, movie, website, or game contains sex, violence, lies, or racism is all but irrelevant. The only factor that has any real influence is whether or not the producers can sell the product.

Michael Powell, chairman of the FCC (Federal Communications Commission), clearly recognizes this fact. The FCC is in charge of keeping indecency off the air. Read Powell chastising ABC for opening its Monday Night Football broadcast with a racy ad promoting the series *Desperate Housewives:* "It would seem to me that while we get a lot of broadcasting companies complaining about indecency enforcement, they seem . . . willing to keep the issue at the forefront, keep it hot and steamy in order to get financial gains and the free advertising it provides."

Sure, some media communicates information and values that are truly useful and beneficial, but these are quite the exception. Instead, the messages it communicates are overwhelmingly ones of greed, lawlessness, conflict, power, self-indulgence, and sexual conquest. The virtues of unselfish love, giving, caring, honesty, peace, patience, and outright kindness are seldom considered marketable and rarely given airtime.

When you look around and see your friends who are struggling — struggling with depression, drugs, aimlessness, or conflicts with people — ask them what shows they watch, what music they listen to, and what games they play. Chances are very good that you'll find the friends experiencing the most problems are also the ones exposing themselves to the worst media influences. The connection between personal struggles and media is unmistakable.

## IN YOUR FACE

On this subject, Ozzy Osbourne got it right: "TV is the most powerful thing that has ever been invented."[1] Kids spend more time watching television and movies than in any other activity except sleep! In fact, 54% of youth have a TV in their bedroom.[2] Let's focus for a moment on what network television, cable TV, and feature movies are pumping into our minds. Once you step back and watch for what's really happening on the screen, you can't help but be alarmed, regardless of your age:

• **Voluminous Violence**

Actor George Clooney realizes the direction TV and movies are heading. "People's misery becoming entertainment, that's what's dangerous. And that seems to be the place we're going. I worry about television."[3] By the time they graduate from high school, most teenagers will have viewed over 200,000 shootings, stabbings, or murders. All in all, the guilty go unpunished in 73 percent of all these violent scenes. One out of four violent altercations involve the use of handguns. Premium cable channels present the highest percentage of violent programs, at 85 percent. By contrast, only 4 percent of programs emphasize an anti-violent theme.[4]

The violence in the media is increasing, and there's a reason behind it. Lt. Col. David Grossman, a U.S. Army Ranger and professor at West Point, knows all about violence. Listen to his take: "Violence is like the nicotine in cigarettes. The reason why the media has to pump ever more violence into us is because we've built up a tolerance. In order to get the same high, we need ever-higher levels. . . . The television industry has gained its market share through an addictive and toxic ingredient."[5]

Even more concerning than the rise in violence is the way people respond to it. Several studies conducted by UCLA "found that children may become 'immune' to the horror of violence; gradually accepting violence as a way to solve problems; imitating the violence they observe on television." With so much violent video exposure, should we really be surprised when kids turn to making explosives, taking guns to school, and even killing one another?

## • Shameless Sex

The average 18 year old has already viewed between 60,000 and 100,000 sexual encounters, and over 90% were with someone other than a husband or wife. Live on a steady diet of MTV, and the numbers are far higher. Victor B. Cline conducted a revealing survey on the movies shown in mainstream theaters in a moderately conservative western city. The following is a summary of the sexual incidents, actions, and situations shown in the 37 motion pictures playing during this period.[6]

Nudity — 168 depictions
Bed scenes with sexual connotations — 49 scenes
Dressing in undergarments with sexual
      contact — 36 scenes
Seductive exhibition of the body — 32 scenes
Verbalizing of sexual interest or intentions
      — 36 scenes
Caressing another's sex organs while clothed
      — 27 scenes
Caressing another's sex organs while nude
      — 21 scenes
Undressing — 34 scenes
Explicit intercourse — 19 scenes
Suggested or implied intercourse — 17 scenes
Homosexual activities — 11 scenes
Oral/genital intercourse — 7 scenes
Rape — 4 scenes
Masturbation — 3 scenes
Sexual sadomasochism — 3 scenes

These are the totals for scenes not from porn movies, but from mainstream, conventional movies. Don't forget, children were a part of the audiences! With so much video modeling of loose and perverted sex, should we really be surprised when kids themselves follow the models they've been shown over and over again?

Not at all. In fact, a scientific study of 1,792 adolescents ages 12–17 showed that watching sex on TV encourages teens to have sex. The more sex they watched, the more likely they were to follow the examples. Kids who watched the most sex were more than twice as likely to indulge in sexual intercourse as those who saw the least amount.[7]

In particular, watching MTV changes the attitudes of young viewers. In 171 hours of MTV programming, researchers found 1,548 sexual scenes containing 3,056 depictions of sex or various forms of nudity, and 2,881 verbal sexual references. This means that kids watching MTV are viewing an average of 9 sexual scenes per hour along with approximately 18 sexual depictions and 17 instances of sexual talk.[8] What is the impact? At least two experiments show that watching MTV results in looser views about sex. One experiment showed that college students who were assigned to watch MTV became more accepting of premarital sex than those who did not watch MTV.[9] The second experiment found that seventh and ninth graders were more likely to approve of premarital sex after watching just one hour of MTV![10]

The tragic deception is that the model of sex portrayed on TV and movies almost never lets you in on the indescribable pain that follows in real life. They don't mention the million unwanted teen pregnancies that happen each year. They don't touch on the resulting sexually transmitted diseases like HIV and herpes. Neither do these scenes reveal the enormous agony over broken vows and relationships, nor the shame and embarrassment that inevitably follows casual sex.

• **Addictive Advertisements**

Beer and other alcohol commercials not only make up a large portion of open advertisements, they are also subtly and intentionally embedded throughout movies and videos. Alcohol advertisers deliberately place their ads on programs that teens watch most, and American teenagers view many thousands of these. What's the impact? Jim O'Hara, of the Center on Alcohol Marketing and Youth at Georgetown University, observed, "Every single day, 7,000 kids under age 16 take their first drink, and $6 billion of alcohol advertising and marketing each year isn't helping."[11]

These ads, of course, never show you the rest of the picture: the messed-up alcoholic, his ruined career, or the car wreck where some little child was slaughtered by a drunk driver. Instead, these commercials play up the themes of alcohol somehow making you sexier, smarter, or more athletic. Wrong! With so much emphasis on drinking in the media, it's a struggle for some teenagers to not take the hint and start to drink anyway.

• **Ubiquitous Occult**

Riddled throughout the entertainment industry are also themes that emphasize witchcraft, sorcery, demon worship, divination, and astrology. We're not talking about just a little magic like in *Beauty and the Beast* or *Snow White and the Seven Dwarfs*. No. We're talking about films that are designed to highlight the power of the occult: *The Grudge, The Ring, Saw, Child's Play,* and *Harry Potter.*

Blood sacrifice, murder, body mutilation, curses, revenge, death, divination, demonic possession, witchcraft, evil charms, consulting with familiar spirits, hexes and magic, wizardry, ghosts, spell casting, sorcery, and new age doctrine are just some of the satanic themes stressed in the *Harry Potter* movies and books. As a result, thousands of kids today are looking for identity in the occult. In fact, the Pagan Federation had to appoint new staff to deal with a flood of inquiries on magic and wizardry following the success of *Harry Potter.*

The greatest tragedy is the influence on individuals like Gioia Bishop, age ten. After watching *Harry Potter* she declared, "I was eager to get to Hogwarts first because I like what they learned there and I want to be a witch."[12] Don't be fooled by the "imaginary strength" or "innocent supernaturalism" of these stories and films. The occult is a very real, and gravely dangerous, force. It intentionally appears subtle and harmless on the surface, but like cocaine addiction, once you are lured and trapped within, the experience is literally hell.

## IN YOUR EARS

If you are like most teenagers, you'll listen to over 150,000 different rock and pop songs by the time you graduate from high school. Some of these bands will become your favorites. You'll memorize their words, share their songs with your friends, and even learn to play them yourself. That's an incredible amount of influence on your life!

What are these songs about? If you pay attention, you'll find that over 99 percent of the lyrics are about "love" and "sex," but the love and sex they are singing about is with a girlfriend or boyfriend, a relative, someone else's wife, someone of the same sex, etc. Less than 1 percent of popular songs today say anything about purity, honesty, and sacrifice being at the heart of real love, and even less about committed, intimate marriage being the scene of the very best sex.

Still, many students who are hooked on rock write off the influence of the lyrics by saying, "I don't even hear the words. I just listen to the music. It has no effect on me." This is exactly the same story we hear from people in the early stages of drinking, smoking pot, and pornography. It never seems harmful in the beginning, but if they could only look ahead a few months! We've seen the depression, suicide, drug addiction, Satan worship, alcoholism, and abortion that can be traced to music's influence. All the while, many teens contest, "It isn't affecting me." How can it not affect you, especially once you understand what most music is about? Let's analyze the themes that are saturated into today's popular music:

• Sex: Distortion to the Max

This entire book could not contain all the examples of totally warped ideas about sex that are fed to young people through music today. What God designed as an exciting, pure, private, and lovely activity between husband and wife has been totally disassembled and corrupted through today's music.

The rapper Ludacris in his song "Area Codes" sings about traveling the world looking for sex. In another song, "What's Your Fantasy?" Ludacris promises to fulfill the most warped dreams one can imagine. Consider the song "Please Don't Hate Me," by Insane Clown Posse (ICP). This one is about a guy having sex with his best friend's mother, but nevertheless he demands, "Please don't hate me, but you never should trust in a friend."

Shaggy's song "It Wasn't Me" boasts about having sex with the girl who lives next door. Lil' Jon & The East Side Boyz boast in their song "Contract" about cruelly selling prostitutes. "Stick That Thing Out" (Skeezer) tells about a woman pulled into oral and group sex. "One Night Stand" lewdly glamorizes infidelity, while "Grand Finale" endorses Kobe Bryant's illicit affair.

Eminem's CD *Encore* starts off with "My 1st Single," singing about oral sex, homosexuality, celebrity porn videos, and sex between people and animals. His graphic "Love You More" endorses promiscuity with lyrics like, "You're a slut, but I'm equal," while "A-- Like That" compares how stimulating various female celebrities' backsides are.

Lest we think that perverted messages like these are confined to rap bands, consider Marilyn Manson's *Mechanical Animals* CD. His song "User Friendly" boasts, "I'm not in love, but I'm gonna f - - - you until someone better comes along." Velvet Revolver's *Contraband* CD includes cuts like "Illegal i Song" that describes bloody fist fights and a sexual encounter with a prostitute. The singer then goes on to describe in "Big Machines" how his wife and kids enslave him!

Listening to messages like these, is it any wonder that many people approach sex with a selfish, can't-get-enough attitude — one that leads to heartbreak, destroyed relationships, disease, humiliation, rape, incest, and endless emotional pain!

## • Sadomasochism: The Ultimate Sexual Perversion

Sadomasochism is the practice of brutally beating a sexual partner during sexual intercourse. Imagine the depravity of the mind that would tell a guy to tie up a girl and start beating, whipping, kicking, or biting her viciously while she gives you what God intended to be a priceless and precious wedding gift! These are the very messages embedded throughout today's music.

Eminem's *Encore* CD expresses the ultimate warped perversion through lyrics like "One minute I wanna slit your throat, then next I want sex." Slipknot's, "The Nameless," from their *The Subliminal Verses* CD, claims, "The only thing I ever really loved was hurting you." Insane Clown Posse details slitting the throat of a lover while singing "Another Love Song" on their *The Amazing Jeckel Brothers* CD.

Imagine how a girl feels when the date is over, and she has been abused by some self-seeking guy who wants to be the villain on every page in her book of dreams! Sure, you may say, I'd never do something like this to a girl. Then why do people listen to the music? How could these bands be so incredibly popular if many people don't resonate with their themes?

### • Violent Vibrations

Some music is known for its good vibrations, but violent themes are the core message embedded within some music. Lil' Jon & The East Side Boyz boast of shooting a rival gangster in the head and watching the blood and brains flow out ("Get Crunk"). Marilyn Mason claims in the song "Fundamentally Loathsome," "If I loved myself I'd be shooting you." Alternatively, he recommends shooting himself in "Mechanical Animals:" "I'm just a boy playing the suicide king." Eminem's *Spend Some Time* CD is marked by images of Eminem shooting people who bought tickets to his concert.

Insane Clown Posse gets the prize for some of the most noxious lyrics in the history of music. They rap about axing people to death, cutting off their heads, and poking out their eyes. Their song "Bring It On" raps about slaying teachers, while "Mad Professor" dramatizes the dissection of 80 people to form a Frankenstein zombie. Perhaps the vilest of all is the song "I Stab People" that describes in vivid detail just how and where he committed these senseless murders. ICP wraps up the song with the confession, "I just wanna talk to you guys about a problem I got. . . . Maybe you can help me." Yes, let's start by taking a hard look at the music with which you are saturating yourself!

Imagine that people are actually promoting and making money by producing and selling music like this! Do their mothers know? How about their sisters?

## • Satanism: The Occult Goes Mainstream

The occult movement is dedicated to the blasphemy of God, and appeals directly to Satan and his demons for power. As further proof that many music producers will do absolutely anything to sell records, they frequently design songs around satanic themes. Consider briefly the evidence of occult influence on today's music.

Nine Inch Nails expresses the assurance that they are on their way to hell:

> And I descend from grace
> in arms of undertow
> I will take my place
> in the great below.

Marilyn Manson assures his alignment with Satan with songs like "Posthuman" that claim, "This isn't god. God is just a statistic," and "The Last Day on Earth" anticipates reincarnation after death. With this personal understanding of God, it's no surprise when Marilyn goes on to sing "I wanna die young and sell my soul" ("I Want to Disappear").

After a few years of disappointing record sales, the aging, failing Rolling Stones realized the key to becoming popular again and selling their pornographic music to the American youth. "Now we're going after the mind," the Stones claimed, and so they did. "Sway" is a song about demon power. "Dancing with Mr. D" is a song about a graveyard romp with the devil, and "Sympathy for the

Devil" is an anthem for many churches of Satan. The rest is history.

It is truly impossible to listen to such lyrics and not be swayed. Saturate your mind with these songs and tragically, like Nine Inch Nails, you too may become convinced there really is nothing better to anticipate than hell itself.

## • Drugs: Acid in Your Ears

Rock music has been the number one public promoter of drugs in the past decades — with no regard for the countless deaths and the imprisoned lives that result from its influence. With another teenager addicted to hard drugs every 43 seconds, you might think that the recording industry would do everything possible to eliminate "drug music" from the air. Instead, just the opposite is happening. They know that addiction to drugs goes hand-in-hand with some music. If they can get people to pay for drugs, how much easier it is to get them to also pay for the music that promotes the habit!

Do you question whether drugs and music are connected? Consider what Jerry Garcia, the worshiped (and now dead) leader of the Grateful Dead, exposed about this truth: "Acid rock is music you listen to when you're high on acid."

Or consider the lyrics of this Metallica song:

Chop your breakfast [cocaine] on a mirror;
Try me and you will see
More is all you need.

Dedicated to how I'm killing you.
Mr. Brown's store I used to do a little [heroin],
But a little won't do it — so the little
Got more and more.

Not to break the foundation laid by earlier bands, several cuts on the Lost Boyz' *Legal Drug Money* CD boasts of marijuana as the group's preferred drug, while "The Yearn" explicitly describes a drug assisted sexual conquest. Not to be outdone, Marilyn Manson plays on the "Devil made me do it" excuse for getting into drugs with titles like "I Don't Like the Drugs, But They Like Me" and "Dope Show." The latter song begins with the anti-drug theme "The drugs they say make us feel so hollow" but then gives way to the declaration "We're all stars now in the dope show."

The music makes drugs sound so good, and the musicians in their "successful" lifestyles try to back up the deception. The reality of their stupidity, however, is seen in the mounting death toll among musicians. As their lies about drugs fill our ears, our parties, our cars, and our homes, the musicians themselves die in their own deception. Some of the best names in popular music have become most remembered for dying by inhaling their own vomit as their bodies convulsed from drugs.

As music's lethal messages about drugs, sex, and Satanism penetrate our culture, so have their deadly effects penetrated countless young lives. Sure, we have all experienced the fact that rock music is easy to get into and hard to turn off. It can make you feel relaxed, and help soothe your worries (besides transforming your car into a four-speaker jam box).

P.O.D. lead singer Sonny Sandoval is wising up to the facts: "I think we've just gotten rid of the whole notion of even a bit of responsibility. You know, there's one thing to be artistic and stuff, but you used to have a conscience about things and a heart about things. . . . I'm almost frightened for the kids of today, but I think everybody's kind of just thrown even a little bit of conscience out the window for entertainment purposes."

So much of today's music is frightening to people like us who love kids, and who carry broken hearts over the subtle brainwashing that is sending much of your generation into the junkyard of broken dreams and shattered lives.

## On Your Game Pad

The explosion of computer technology in the 1990s is one of the biggest developments in modern history. Computer games — a vivid example of this technology — have taken our nation by storm. Almost every kid has easy access to them, whether for PCs, PlayStation, Game Boy, or others. Some of these games are truly fun and wholesome, even educational, but here's the rub: The majority of top-selling computer games are built around the same destructive themes that dominate movies and music. Consider just a few of the most popular games on the market today:

**Halo** — This fast paced adventure is built around killing alien creatures as fast as they appear. Some aliens look remarkably human and spill blood just as any person would. Show any hesitation — as a thought of compassion might inspire — and the player winds up dead.

**Grand Theft Auto 3** — The players work for the Mafia. Their job as Mafia agents is to steal cars and kill people that are targeted by the Mafia. Drive by shootings, pimping for prostitutes, and killing police officers all add points to the player's winning total.

**Doom** — Contestants in this game are to use plasma guns, rocket launchers, and chainsaws to destroy demonic creatures unleashed from hell. The dialogue includes, "You will die, and your soul will be mine," "Death will not be your end. Your soul will burn in hell forever," and "I will bring hell on earth." Violent depictions include a demon exploding from within a woman's head, and a still-wriggling decapitated human body.

**Half Life** — As the physicist defending the world from invading aliens, the player stops at nothing, including killing other humans. Blowing up generic soldiers, killing zombies, and crashing cars leaves the players gasping in fear and firing their weapons blindly at anything that moves.

**Resident Evil** — In the course of a game, the player guns down hundreds of enemies, if he or she is not in turn cleaved, crushed, or swallowed by a demonic opponent. Several locations within the game resemble morgues filled with bloody bodies, or piles of humans as if just executed.

**Nine Things Teens Should Know**

Check out this promotional review of a new game in a leading video game magazine:

Crave's newest offering, Galerians, is an acid drop in the Survival Horror genre pioneered by Resident Evil. It begins in a dreadful hospital, with inhuman scientists experimenting on a restrained and unwilling young boy. Fittingly horrible, and the game never lets up from there. In fact, it gets much worse. With a gut-gnarling story line about a telekinetic child, cyborg test subjects who hunt him, PPEC drugs that provide our hero with his only defense while at the same time eating away his body, a computer with a mind hell-bent against humanity, and a pitiless society that welcomes their murder, this game is adult entertainment. It's darker than black, gleefully indulging in sin.

Sure, we all acknowledge that these games are "make-believe," but it's impossible to deny that those who spend hours each week hunting and killing "imaginary" people are not adversely affected themselves. Similarly, kids and adults who saturate their minds with the occult — even if it's "all in fun" — have opened themselves up to an evil more powerful than they can ever imagine.

Listen to the words of Terrance Stone, a youth leader and former gang member, on how violent video games such as Grand Theft Auto have glamorized the gang lifestyle:

**Nicholas Comninellis & Joe White**

I have been to something like 50 gang funerals where the guy in the coffin was no more than 20. The game companies don't see the family crying and the people in the coffin. They don't see the impact this has on our culture. They make or play their games in the studio, but for kids on the street it's a real life.

The video game industry rakes in seven billion dollars a year selling ever more realistic experiences to teenagers — experiences that highlight killing, theft, destruction, and satanic power. The power of these games is compounded by peer pressure that says they are just an innocent diversion. Whatever captures your attention, whatever occupies your mind, eventually saturates your heart.

## AT YOUR FINGERTIPS

The Internet is another terrific example of computer power at our fingertips — one that can be used for awesome good, and also one that can be twisted into an instrument of devastation. Nowhere is this more obvious than in the Internet's ability to deliver pornography.

Pornography basically means graphic pictures and videos showing people undressed and engaged in sexual behavior. The stuff is very addictive, especially to men. Once they start looking at it, and getting sexually excited over the images, it can be very hard for them to break the habit. People in the pornography industry know this is true, and are making billions of dollars each year by selling men access to pornographic photos, movies, and magazines.

Today, the Internet has supercharged the pornography world by making it so easy for anyone, even kids, to find these pictures. Pornographic websites are designed very seductively. They start out showing girls in bikinis and lingerie, then as the user surfs through the websites, the girls have on less and less. Then the website lures the user with the line, "Wanna see these girls nude? Just put in your credit card number and for only $20 a month. . . ." You get the idea.

Sexual desire is a good, God-given quality, but pornography takes all that is right about sex and corrupts it. Instead of sex being a gift that couples "give" to one another, pornography is all about "getting" sex at any cost. Instead of sex being a private, intimate experience between two who deeply love each other, pornography promotes sex as an instinct to be followed with anyone, at anytime, anywhere, in any way.

Someday you will be sorely tempted. You'll be at a friend's house and he'll say, "Hey, wanna see this hot website?" Or, you'll be alone and be lured to go to a search engine to type in sexually provocative words and go to the websites that come up.

Why are we telling you all this? So you'll be prepared; so that when the temptation comes you'll know what to do. The truth is that guys really want to be free from porn. We've never met a boy or man who actually likes the addiction, who is proud of what it is doing to him, who feels more satisfied because of it all. They wish instead they had never given into temptation.

- What is the main reason why producers and advertisers push violent or sexually provocative entertainment?

- How does viewing violence over the long run affect the thinking of a person?

- What are the sexual values most often communicated through the media? Which of these are actually wholesome?

- How do you think the occult displayed in videos and games compares with satanic power itself?

- How can you tell when a video, song, or game starts to cross the line into what is unhealthy?

- What standards do you set for yourself regarding the entertainment that you use?

## FOR TEEN EYES ONLY

Listen carefully. Video, movies, music, games, and the Internet are not in themselves evil or wrong. We enjoy a delightful movie or moving song just as much as anyone else, but media is extremely powerful, and is often used for evil purposes. Your job as a teen, and your parent's responsibility as an adult, is to evaluate the quality of what you put in your face, your ears, and at your fingertips. Learn to say no to what will harm you, and to appreciate what will make you a better person.

It is absolutely impossible to surround yourself with messages about drugs, sex, violence, and the occult, and then not be injured. Tear after tragic tear is shed as we talk to teenagers and young singles that still hurt and suffer because they were influenced by what they watched and listened to.

You become what you think about. You become what you see. You become what you hear. You "create" your own personality and character by the input you give your inner "computer." You can stuff it with an arsenal of self-destructive grenades, or you can make it a storehouse full of supplies and tools to build an internal mansion of joy and strength and peace.

This is exactly why the Bible urges us to be careful what we put in our minds:

> Finally, whatever is true, whatever is honorable, whatever is lovely, whatever is of good repute, if there is any excellence and if anything worthy of praise, let your mind dwell on these things (Phil. 4:8; NASB).

Make a decision for yourself to be different from the crowd. Instead of going along with whatever entertainment your friends prefer, ask yourself honestly whether or not it will be good for you. Reject anything questionable. Expose yourself only to what is excellent.

Picture your mind as a fortress. A mental image of a castle from a medieval movie would be ideal. The battle plan of the invading army is to find a weak spot in the wall, break through, and conquer the city. If the army is successful, it will mean tragedy for those inside. No wonder the walls are built as strong as possible, and manned with all of the toughest soldiers in the city!

In the case of corrupt entertainment, the invaders are not clothed in armor, nor do they carry spears. They may not appear dangerous at all. In fact, they may be incredibly attractive, tempting you lay down your defenses, open the gates, and welcome them inside!

Don't do it!

Every little kid in America can tell you about the Battle of the Alamo. Many even remember the tales of Davy Crockett, Jim Bowie, Colonel William Travis, and their bigger-than-life commitment to the independence of Texas from Mexico.

As the battle intensified, the now-famous 180 heroes dug in to defend the mission against the assaults by Santa Anna's huge army, and realized there was no escape. Colonel Travis called his band of soldiers to the sandy ground of the Alamo floor. There he drew his sword and struck a line into San Antonio's dust as he boldly proclaimed their life-and-death choice. "We're buying precious time for Sam Houston to prepare the Texas Army for the upcoming battle for Texas's independence. Every day we hold out against Santa Anna is 24 invaluable hours of training . . . our effort will be known in history as the difference between Sam Houston's victory or defeat!"

Then Colonel Travis looked squarely into the eyes of his 179 men and declared, "In the final days of this battle, every man who stays with me will surely die." The pages of history ring with his final declaration, "You who wish to die like heroes and patriots come over to me and step over this line. You who choose to leave stay where you are."

At first, no one dared a step. Then one brave soul stepped across the line . . . then there were two, three, four, and more. When Crockett made his move, he was joined by more than a dozen. Jim Bowie was so sick that he had to be carried across on a stretcher. Soon 178 men joined Travis and made the choice to stand, to defend, to die, to go down in history with "Remember the Alamo!"

Will you step across the line today? Will you make a commitment to guard your mind against the sly powers of the entertainment world? Will you take a stand against any music, movie, or technology that contains messages of sex, violence, drugs, or Satanism? Do so and you'll not only protect your own life, you'll also go down in history as one of the smartest, most disciplined — and ultimately happy — teens in your generation!

**Notes**

1. *USA Today,* June 10, 2003,D1-2.

2. A.C. Huston and J.C. Wright, University of Kansas, "Television and Socialization of Young Children," in Tannis M. MacBeth, editor, *Tuning in to Young Viewers* (Thousand Oaks, CA: Sage, 1996).

3. Quoted by Reuters, February 11, 2003.

4. National Violence Study, February 1996, Mediascope, Inc.

5. Lt. Col. David Grossman, U.S. Army (Ret.) Ranger, quoted in the *Arizona Republic*, May 27, 1999, by Tim Madigan, *Fort Worth Star-Telegram*, A18.

6. Dr. Victor B. Cline, "Pornography's Effect on Adults and Children," *Morality in Media*, December 12, 2001.

7. Rebecca L. Collins, Marc N. Elliott, Sandra H. Berry, et al., "Watching Sex on Television Predicts Adolescent Initiation of Sexual Behavior," *Pediatrics*, Sept 2004; 114: e280–e289.

8. Casey Williams, "MTV Smut Peddlers: Targeting Kids with Sex, Drugs and Alcohol. A Report on MTV Programming." March 20, 2004–March 27, 2004, by Parents Television Council.

9. M.S. Calfin, J.L. Carroll, and J. Schmidt, "Viewing Music-Video Tapes before Taking a Test of Premarital Sexual Attitudes," *Psychological Reports*, 72, (1993): 475-481.

10. L.E. Greeson and R.A. Williams, "Social Implications of Music Videos on Youth: An Analysis of the Content and Effects of MTV," *Youth and Society*, 18 (1986): 177–189.

11. Press release, October 12, 2004, Georgetown University.

12. "What Readers Think About Goblet?" *San Francisco Chronicle*, 7–26.

"...your parents **deeply want** to be close to you, too."

**9** Nine Things
Countdown to Adolescence

**Chapter**

**7**

# Getting Along With Parents

## GETTING TO THE CORE

Your parents were once adolescents. Though it was quite a while ago, they still remember what it was like, but they may have trouble putting into words what they learned as teenagers. During this period in your life, your parents will likely want to share with you some of their own adolescent experiences. They may have never, ever put these into words before, so be patient with your mom or dad.

You may also discover that it's difficult to talk with your parents, especially about certain sensitive or emotional subjects. Yet you may also feel like you really want them to know what's going on inside of you. These conflicting sentiments are normal. In time, you'll find the right moment to share your feelings, so be both patient with yourself and ready to share when that moment seems natural.

Friends are incredibly important during adolescence, but your connection with your parents, while changing in character, also remains critical to your happiness during the teenage years. After all, we're talking about those two people who brought you into this world — the pair who changed your diaper 10,000 times, who cleaned up countless messes after you, who labored with you over homework and school projects, and who have felt more pain over you and enjoyed more laughs with you than you'll ever realize. They are an enormous part of your life's history.

Maybe you have only one parent now, or perhaps some proud grandparents or adoptive parents have taken over the role. Nevertheless, as a child you probably enjoyed spending lots of time with your parents, but as you progress through adolescence you will find that you don't need as much time with them as before. In fact, by the time most kids are teens, they take their parent's love and advice so much for granted that it's almost a crime.

An illustration of this neglect for parental advice was revealed in an extensive survey that showed 80% of teenagers in America would still spend time with a particular friend, even if their parents disapproved. We've lost count of the number of brokenhearted teenagers we know who disregarded their parent's companionship and their advice, traveled down the wrong road, and got hurt on the way.

## An Angel In Hell

One lost traveler was Angel. She fell for Gil, a handsome guy who was three years older than her. Gil had some problems, she knew for sure. He was into pornography and smoking pot, and he hadn't held down a job in over six months. Gil had no interest in God, but never stopped trying to interest Angel in sleeping with him. Nevertheless, Angel thought that if she gave in to Gil he would change.

Angel's dad tried to put an end to the relationship because he could see she was going to get hurt. He tried to get through to Angel, but she wouldn't listen to his opinion. Angel's mom would invite some of Angel's other friends over to visit, but Angel would first sneak out of the house to see Gil. Eventually she ran off with him and got married.

For weeks, Angel completely disappeared. Not a word did she communicate to her parents. Then, 11 horrible months later, Angel appeared at their front door. Her eyes were sunken, her hair tangled, and her chin swollen and disfigured — evidence of a broken jaw from where the guy's angry fist had struck. Angel's dad and mom pulled her inside, into their arms, and back into the love that helped Angel patch up her shattered life.

## Declaration Of Independence

Angel is a more glaring example of the disconnection that can happen between teens and their parents. Nevertheless, some degree of "conflict between generations" is unavoidable during adolescence. Why? Because making increasingly independent choices is an essential part of your growth during the teenage years, and your parents will not always agree with the choices you make.

As a child, your parents gave you certain freedoms, depending upon your abilities. In the beginning, they walked you to the bus stop. Then, when they were confident you knew the way, they let you go on your own. Later, your parents allowed you to ride your bike to school with them following in the car. After they were assured you wouldn't get lost, they let you ride alone or with friends. Soon, you'll ask your parents to let you drive a car to school. They will consider this, but only when they are certain about your capabilities behind the wheel.

You may believe you're ready to drive to school (or go on dates, or stay out late, or get a job) long before your parents do. As a result, tempers may flare, harsh words may be exchanged, and everybody inevitably feels badly.

Of course, disagreements over your freedoms have been going on ever since your were a toddler and tried to play in the refrigerator. What's different about adolescence is that your abilities are growing far more rapidly — but you're still not quite ready to live on your own. So what you can and can't do, what you're allowed and not allowed to do, require constant negotiations between yourself and your parents.

## HEART OF THE MATTER

This conflict over privileges and freedoms is the main cause of distance that teenagers and parents feel between one another. We hear story after story from kids who feel like their parents are "just being mean" or are "too hard" on them, as well as from parents who believe their kids are always "pushing the limits" and "not respecting the rules."

Deep down inside, neither parents nor their kids want conflict between each other. They do not desire open confrontation, nor silent retreat, nor simply playing "make believe" that everything is okay when it's not.

Instead, what teens and parents want most in their heart of hearts is to respect each other, enjoy activities together, build terrific memories, and get ready for the day when teens will be fully prepared to live independently. This particular 15 year old expressed it well:

> I need to talk to you about my parents. I do obey them with somewhat of a smile. It's really hard, though, because I really don't "feel" much love for my parents. I mean, sometimes I can't control my thoughts and feelings toward them. Still, I wish I could get the feeling that I would love to do stuff with them again.

Just like this kid, if you look deep within yourself, you'll also discover an incredible affection — one that can only result from the extraordinary bond shared by a teen and parent. You may not "feel" this bond all the time, maybe not even very often, but rest assured that it is in your heart.

Young people, your parents deeply want to be close to you, too. They may not know how to express this very clearly. Their timing may be way off. They may seem tongue-tied, uneasy, or clumsy, but you alone mean more to your mom and dad than anything on earth. If fact, this is one of the reasons they are probably the ones who suggested this book to you!

**Nicholas Comninellis & Joe White**

## Coming Back Home

Just because you're becoming more independent does not mean you have to sacrifice your relationship with your parents. While some distance is probably inevitable, much of it can be shrunk and you can start right now to rediscover and to enjoy your parents again. Here are some practical things you can do:

### • Be thankful to your parents

Express gratefulness for everything they do for you at the time it happens. Adolescence can be a very difficult time for parents. Try to thank them at least five times every day. You'd be surprised how easy it is to find five things to thank them for. If you're sharp, you can find almost a hundred! Notes and letters are an especially powerful way to communicate your appreciation.

I (Joe) learned one of the greatest lessons in my life about being thankful one day when my six-year-old daughter asked me to help her build a toy wagon out of wood blocks, using hickory nuts for wheels. I was busy at the moment, but this seemed a neat opportunity to spend time with my girl. We got the wagon 80% finished that afternoon, and then took a break to let the glue dry. I thought we'd get around to finishing it in a day or two, but I was wrong.

That night as I headed for bed, dead-tired and ready to crash, I saw a little note taped on my closet door. In a six-year-old's print (different size letters, slanted lines, and the rest) it read:

I love you, Daddy. Thanks for taking time to make my wagon. Love, Corky

I almost cried. After I showed my wife the note, I ran up to the shop, grabbed the little wagon, and worked tirelessly until it was complete.

Because Corky took time to thank me for what little I had done, I wanted to finish it for her. The next morning the wood block wagon was waiting by her plate when she came to breakfast.

My daughter's simple thanks did wonders to motivate me to give her my all. Try it on your parents. I believe you'll be impressed with the results!

## • Tell your parents often that you love them

Anne was 14. She came to me (Joe) at camp with a deep personal problem. To make a long story short, she told me how she had lost all her happiness. Anne said she just felt rotten all the time. After I had listened for quite a while, she mentioned that she hadn't told her parents she loved them in over three years. Anne knew they needed to hear it, but she found it very hard to tell them. After we talked more, Anne said she'd write them that day and let them know she loved them.

The next day Anne was all smiles. It was as if someone had lifted a hundred-ton weight off her back. "How could writing a letter, something so little, make such a great change in me?" she asked. "I feel like a different person inside." Maybe it wasn't as little a thing as she thought!

## • Listen to your parents with an open mind

Your mom and dad may just be wiser than you think. This 17 year old paints a clear picture of how he discovered this truth the hard way:

As I was growing up, my parents always told me to stay away from drugs. I didn't know then that alcohol is a drug, too. I started drinking in seventh grade. All my friends were doing it, so I joined in the "fun." Actually it is very sad. People don't realize at the time what they're getting into. I sure didn't!

About a year later I was introduced to marijuana. I always wondered what it was like, and again, all the kids were doing it so I had to be "cool" and smoke pot with them. Now I wish I had listened to my parents. Every time I got high I would say to myself, "Just one more time won't hurt." But one more time led to many more times.

Then my brother got me into something totally different — speed. He told me it was fun and would make me happy. So along with drinking and smoking, I was now on speed, too. I liked it, so I kept it up. Then I got to where all that stuff wasn't enough. I needed a better high. Some guy sold me a hit of acid. I had no idea what it would do to me. My friends and I would also smoke joints laced with PCP. Some friends! They wouldn't accept me for who I was. They only liked me if I would get high with them.

I began to skip school, ignore curfews, and didn't obey my parents at all. I couldn't figure out why they didn't leave me alone and let me live my

**Nicholas Comninellis & Joe White**

own life. I had no real friends. I began to get so depressed I wanted to die.

So one night when life seemed hopeless, I actually did it — something I had been thinking about for a long time. I sat down in my room and took a razor blade to my wrist. It wasn't until blood was going all over the place that I knew I didn't want to die. My mother rushed me to the hospital.

When I got out I realized that drugs are not the way to live. I always knew God was with me and would never let me go. I prayed all the time for Him to save me from this nightmare. Now I have a purpose in life. I have been off drugs for four months. I was one of the lucky ones. Through a lot of help and lot of pain, I was able to kick the habit. Now I have new friends, real friends, and I realize that my parents really were right all along.

This teen's parents tried to prevent him from getting into drugs. Imagine the pain he would have avoided if he'd followed their timely advice!

These are just three simple ways to improve or rebuild the link with your parents — simple, but enormously powerful! Give them a try, even when you don't feel in the mood. You'll be impressed with the results!

## THE KEY TO GREATER FREEDOM

Want more independence from your parents? Almost every teen does! We're about to share with you the time-tested, totally proven secret to receiving the freedom you desire.

First, let's look at it from your parent's perspective. Their God-given job is to care for you and train you to be prepared for the adult world, as the proverb admonishes: "Train up a child in the way he should go, and when he is grown he will not depart from it" (Prov. 22:6; NASB). Most parents take this responsibility quite seriously. They are willing to do almost anything possible to help you grow strong and be equipped for life, and nothing gives them more happiness than to see you make progress!

Parents also realize that the kind of care and guidance you need changes significantly as you enter the teenage years. While still accountable to your parents, they must also give you greater freedoms to make some decisions for yourself. This is the only way you can gain experience and develop your own judgment and decision-making skills.

With increasing freedom comes increasing responsibility, and here is the key secret: Only as you prove yourself responsible with new freedoms can you expect more to be added over time.

For example, let's say that you believe you should have the freedom to finish your homework whenever you want, but your parents are still insisting that everything be done before you go out with friends, watch TV, or chat online. Your parents might be willing to give you a trial period during which you can prove to them that you can study whenever you wish, and still keep up your grades, but if you fail to perform, you can (and should) expect a return to the former homework rules.

**Nicholas Comninellis & Joe White**

Want the freedom to do your homework whenever you wish? Prove to your parents you will keep your grades up. Want the privilege of going out with friends? Prove to your parents that you will be home on time. Want the freedom to use your Dad's tools? Demonstrate that you'll put them back when you're finished. Want the freedom to drive a car? Show your parents what an excellent driver you can be. Over time, as you are faithful with new privileges, new ones will inevitably be added. It will make both you and your parents extremely happy!

If you find your parents are not giving you enough freedom, the best way to handle things is to simply sit down and discuss it. Tell them you feel you are old enough to make more choices for yourself. Listen to their concerns. Negotiate with them. Promise you'll carry through on your responsibilities, then make good on your promises. Realize that sometimes you'll also have to take no for an answer — no matter how faithful you've been so far.

The day after my (Nicholas') 16th birthday, the Beach Boys were playing a concert at the football stadium in Kansas City. I had planned out the entire weekend. I'd take (and pass) my driver's test on Friday. Then, on Saturday afternoon, I'd pick up my date (whose parents were nervous about me behind the wheel), and drive her to the stadium (where the traffic was always horrendous).

When I presented my plan to Mom and Dad, however, I got a thumbs down. My father had taken me driving many times, and knew well my limitations. I was still running off the left-hand side of the road, screeching my tires when I accelerated, and unsure what to do at intersections. Even if I passed the driver's examination, it would clearly be weeks before I was up to the challenge of driving in congested traffic.

I was heartbroken with their decision and I wept with bitter disappointment, but Dad was right. My abilities were not yet up to the privilege of driving to the concert. Six months later, the Doobie Brothers came to town. I just loved their music, and approached my parents again about driving to the concert. By this time, I could keep the car in the middle of the lane, gently accelerate without spinning the wheels, and confidently take my turn at intersections. Dad looked at my mom, and replied, "Sure, Son, you can go. You want to take my car this time?"

## WHAT DO YOU THINK?

- Why does it feel awkward to talk to your parents about personal things you are feeling?

- What do you suppose is different about being a teenager now compared with when your parents were kids?

- What is the main source of conflict between parents and teens?

- What can you especially thank your parents for today?

- Why is telling your parents you love them good for your own mental health?

- What is some advice your parents recently gave you that you should listen to again?

**Nicholas Comninellis & Joe White**

- What is the key to gaining greater personal freedom from your parents?

The safest, most effective course toward independence is a path made up of gradually adding new privileges, developing and proving yourself all along the way. Sound like work? It is! It would seem far easier for your parents to say, "Just go do whatever you want. Go to school if you please. Do your homework only if you're in the mood. I'll feed you whenever you're around and never ask you about anything that might upset you." That would be a simple (and simplistic) way to avoid all conflicts.

True love, and your parent's deep affection for you, demands the longer, more careful journey. The case of John Walker Lindh is striking. You'll remember he's the young American who ended up fighting on the side of the Taliban army in Afghanistan. John was captured with an assault rifle in a battle wherein a U.S. soldier was killed. John Walker Lindh was charged with treason against America.

How does an American kid wind up in a foreign army battling against his homeland? A glaring indication of John Walker's road to treason was the role of his parents. John Walker's mother and father were very lax in their approach to training, preferring to give him few guidelines and to let young John Walker "discover his own way in life." In California, he attended what's described as an elite alternative high school, where students were allowed to shape their own studies however they wished. In his mid teens, John Walker read the autobiography of Malcolm X (a radical and violent leader of the Nation of Islam organization), which sparked John Walker's conversion to Islam. His parents supported the decision.

John Walker studied the Koran, adopted a Moslem name, and started wearing a long white robe and a turban. In 1998, John Walker asked his parents for money to go to Yemen. He said it was the best country to learn the "pure" dialect of Arabic used in the Koran. Again, his parents were completely behind him.

Eventually, John Walker made his way to Pakistan, where he enrolled in a paramilitary training camp run by a militant group. Soon thereafter, John Walker ventured to Afghanistan, where he joined the Taliban. He told a *Newsweek* reporter that he entered Afghanistan "to help the Islamic government . . . because the Taliban are the only government that actually provides Islamic law." As needed, his parents kept sending money to support John Walker's self-chosen lifestyle.

Next, the young American was sent to an Al-Qaeda training camp, where he is said to have met Osama Bin Laden, who thanked John Walker for taking part in the jihad (holy war) against America — the "war" which claimed some 3,000 innocent lives (including hundreds of children) in the worst act of terrorism in American history on September 11, 2001.

On the inside, whether they realize it or not, every teenager wants the training necessary to prepare themselves for life. The direction and discipline that John Walker

Lindh's parents would not give him, he sought out and received from the Taliban.

Now, fortunately, you'll never have to do anything nearly as radical as John Walker to get training for life. Your parents are right here and ready to do whatever it takes. The world can be a cold, lonely, and dangerous place without the support of a loving family, so take complete advantage of the affection, teaching, and experience of your mom and dad. They are a resource that will bring deep joy and enduring success to your life.

"Be happy
with the physical changes that are taking place
inside of you! "

**9** **Nine Things**
Countdown to Adolescence

# 8

# Total Body Makeover

## GETTING TO THE CORE

We all grow up knowing that boys' and girls' bodies are built differently from one another. Usually, somewhere between 10 and 12 years of age these differences increase dramatically, and it's obvious that our bodies are going through a total makeover.

Your parents, relatives, or friends may point out some of these changes even before you notice them. They may comment that your voice is lower or your shoulders are broader. Or, you look in the mirror one day and suddenly observe some differences for yourself. Carl wrote about this experience:

When I was a kid, I was kind of overweight. I would tighten my belt to the point of strangulation to keep in my tummy. With the same point in mind, I'd insist that my parents buy pants that were way too tight. Every few weeks I'd lock the bathroom door and stand in front of the mirror. I'd look at the size of the bulge on my waist, and pledge to not ever eat ice cream again.

The summer following fifth grade, my family was particularly busy with weekend trips to the lake. We spent the days skiing, swimming, and yes, eating ice cream. For a time, I was so occupied with catching squirrels and learning to ski that I forgot all about my physical appearance.

Just before school started back up again, I sneaked into the bathroom once more to appraise the shape of my body. I locked the door, stripped off my shirt, lifted my arms behind my head, glanced in the mirror, and let out a cry of shock! Something incredible had happened to me! Gone was the little belly I used to carry around. Gone was the self-inflicted belt mark that was once embedded around my waist.

That's not all I discovered. There was a bulge in my upper arms, a ripple across my abdomen, and grooves in my leg muscles. I could hardly believe this image in the mirror was actually my own. How did this possibly happen; and without any effort on my part?

## Master Clock

In Greenwich, England, sits the world's master watch — the single clock that sets the time for all other clocks on earth. Similarly, each of our brains houses its own master clock. It's a tiny organ called the pituitary gland.

This marvelous part of the brain recognizes when it's time for your body to start changing. At the right moment, the pituitary starts putting out hormones — tiny chemicals that travel throughout your body. These hormones act as messengers who signal when it's time to physically "grow up."

While the pituitary is a powerful little organ — capable of totally morphing your body — it's also rather mild-mannered. The pituitary will not overwhelm you all at once with physical maturity. Rather, it causes your body to transform over a period of months or years at a time, and with good reason. Your body has an incredible adjustment to go through!

• Up and away

One of the earliest physical changes of adolescence for both boys and girls is a jump in height, and increase in the size of your body. This is sometimes called a "growth spurt." You'll find that over a period of weeks or months your clothes and shoes are tighter or shorter than they used to be. The muscles of your shoulders, arms, and legs become more full and stout. You start to catch up with your parent's height, and may even become taller than them.

Girls usually begin growing taller before boys do. In the early stages of adolescence they may also seem more athletic and physically coordinated. These facts cause some boys to wonder whether something is wrong with them, but don't worry. Within two or three years, boys usually begin to catch up with their female counterparts.

## • Where's the beef?

With all the growing on the inside, it's no wonder that kids going through adolescence have greater appetites than before. Breakfast goes from being one bowl of cereal into two or three bowls full. Dinner becomes two plates of spaghetti instead of one. Your parents may start making comments about you "eating them out of house and home."

The ferocious teenage appetite is completely normal. Your body is simply demanding more nutrition to support all the new internal construction. So go ahead and give yourself the raw materials you need.

Remember a word of caution, though. Be sure to fill yourself up with healthy foods: with fruits, pasta, vegetables, rice, milk, fish, and bread, for example. Keep yourself away from too much candy, chips, burgers, cheese, ice cream, and other junk foods. A healthy diet will not only give your body the nutrition it needs to grow, but also help you prevent obesity and all the physical and social problems that go along with it.

## • "X" marks the spot

Skin changes also affect both adolescent boys and girls. The skin of your face, in particular, becomes more oily. This oil causes the skin to be more easily infected by bacteria. The result can be acne, blemishes, and pimples. Most teenagers have mild acne at least some time or other.

Occasionally, acne can be quite severe — causing pain, scars, and embarrassment.

Fortunately, it is possible to successfully combat acne. Regular face washing with a quality, bactericidal soap is the first step. You can buy acne preparations (containing benzolperoxide) at any grocery store or pharmacy, and apply them to your skin as directed to kill bacteria. If these fail to work well enough, your doctor can also prescribe more potent acne medications.

• **Where's the bed?**

A fourth characteristic common to teenage boys and girls is a frequent feeling of fatigue. While you once seemed to have boundless energy — able to be active nonstop for hours — adolescence usually brings with it a greater need for sleep. You may find that instead of running outside after school, all you want to do is go to your room

and collapse into bed. Instead of going out on weekends like before, you now prefer to just hang around the house and do nothing. Trish discovered this:

> When I was 11, my mother promised that by the time I was 13, I could stay up until 11 o'clock each night. I so looked forward to being able to chat with my friends and be the last to sign off, but by seventh grade I just couldn't do it anymore, no matter who was online. I'd have to crash into bed. I searched for excuses to go to sleep even earlier than before. I felt so tired I simply had no choice.

When you find yourself growing more tired than usual, remember this is a natural part of adolescence. Give your body the freedom to slow down. Spread out, or even call off some of your activities. Put in at least eight hours of sleep each night. You may even need ten hours to feel truly rested.

The time you invest in sleeping is not wasted. Think of it. When a road is being constructed, it's usually closed to traffic. Cars driving down the middle would make it impossible for the workers to complete the project. Similarly, sleep gives your body the down time that's essential for constructing and developing in even more amazing ways.

• Hair, hair everywhere

As children, we have soft, lighter colored hair covering a few parts of our bodies — mostly arms and legs.

With the onset of adolescence, this hair becomes darker and thicker. It also begins to take on an adult-like pattern. The starting time and intensity of this hair growth, of course, varies from person to person, but most people eventually experience the following changes.

For boys, hair grows on the lower half of your face — starting above your upper lip, then on your chin and cheeks, on front of your neck, and under your arms. Hair may appear on your chest, abdomen, and back. For girls, mature hair begins to grow under your arms, and may also appear on the legs where there was none before. Whether boy or girl, you'll also notice hair growing around your penis or labia.

In the beginning, you may even feel uneasy or even ashamed about the new hair covering your body, but with time, you'll come to adjust to the changes. You many even feel proud of your new hairy look.

## • Voice of change

As adolescence progresses, your voice changes in quality, becoming deeper and fuller in its tone. While girl's voices certainly go through this transition, the effect is most noticeable among boys. One summer, your voice may sound like a flute or clarinet, for example, and then by the following summer, you sound like a bass guitar or tuba.

One's voice often gets a little unsteady during this changeover period. You may find that it "squeaks" or "cracks" from time to time when you try to talk. Your voice may sound as though you have a head cold or feel stuffed up. In addition to the irritation all this brings with it, people around you may also point out how strange your voice sounds — making the transition even more unbearable.

The good news is that the period of unsteadiness in your voice usually only lasts a few weeks or months. While you may feel tempted to keep your mouth shut, lest you embarrass yourself, you will no doubt come through this transition with a beautiful voice you can enjoy the rest of your life.

## HUMAN REPRODUCTION 101

Other physical changes in adolescence have to do with sexual maturity — making your body ready to reproduce a child of your own. A technical word for this time of sexual development is "puberty." Of course, you are years away from having a child. Nevertheless, adolescence is the time when the pituitary gland signals for sexual changes within your body that make reproduction possible.

To grasp the point of some physical changes that are happening, you first need to understand the basics of how human reproduction works. A baby is created when a special tiny cell from a man, called a "sperm," comes in contact with another special cell from a woman, called an "egg." These two cells combine to form the first, original cell of the new baby.

A man's sperm is formed inside his "testicles." These are the two "balls" located within a man's scrotum. The sperm is contained in a white liquid, called "semen." The sperm and semen travel through a tube from the testicles up to and out of the man's penis.

How do the sperm and egg come into contact? It's through an act called "sexual intercourse." This is normally a very enjoyable experience shared between a husband and wife. The man inserts his penis into the opening between a woman's legs, called her "vagina." During sexual intercourse, the man's sperm exit from the tip of the man's penis and enter the woman's vagina. This pumping of sperm from the penis is termed "ejaculation."

Once inside the vagina, the microscopic-size sperm swim up through the opening at the far end of the vagina called the "cervix," and then enter into the woman's "uterus." Inside the uterus, the sperm may come in contact with the woman's egg, and a new baby will be formed, or "conceived."

Where did the woman's egg come from? The woman's egg is originally produced in an organ called the "ovary." Once each month, one of the two ovaries releases an egg, which travels down a passage way called the "fallopian tube," and arrives inside the uterus.

If sperm are waiting there, one of them will combine with the egg to form the first cell of a new baby, and the woman becomes "pregnant." The baby will grow inside her uterus for nine months. When the baby is ready to be born, the cervix — located between the uterus and the vagina — opens up. The baby, which usually weighs six to eight pounds by now, is then pushed out by the uterus, into the vagina, and then out from the vagina's opening between the woman's legs.

**Nicholas Comninellis & Joe White**

If the sperm are not already present in the uterus, the egg will wait there for a few days. If no sperm appear, then the egg and the other cells lining the inside of the uterus will peel off and flow out of the uterus and into the vagina, appearing as a small amount of blood between the woman's legs. This normal process is called menstruation, and it usually occurs about once each month.

These are the basic facts about human reproduction. This entire subject is really sensitive and is often hard for both parents and children to discuss. You will naturally have questions you feel awkward about asking your mom or dad, and your parents will have answers they feel awkward about expressing to you. Yet your parents are the ideal people to help you learn about this subject. Show special understanding and patience with each other. Ask questions. Share answers. In time, the awkwardness will lessen, and you'll be glad you can explore these subjects together.

In the next two sections, we'll talk about the unique sexual maturity that goes on within both boys and girls — the changes that are necessary for them to become adults capable of reproducing like we've just described.

## MALE MATURITY

Boys, you'll begin to notice particular developments that will turn your body into that of an adult male. Your penis will gradually grow in size. So will your testicles. The scrotum that holds them will become larger and more rough or wrinkled in appearance. This is completely normal.

Occasionally, you will notice your penis becoming harder, longer, and thicker — especially while you are in bed. This usually lasts for 5–10 minutes at a time, and may come and go over the course of an evening. This firming of the penis is called an "erection." You may find that during an erection your penis has a special, tingling sensation to it that feels good to you. The purpose of erections is to make your penis solid enough to enter a woman's vagina at the time of sexual intercourse. Erections can occur at almost anytime, and may potentially cause some embarrassment if they happen to you in public. Just remember that erections are entirely normal. It's just your body's way of maturing and preparing for intercourse later in life.

Another event that sometimes bothers boys during adolescence is the occurrence of "wet dreams." This is when the semen is ejaculated from a boy's penis without him knowing it. Some adolescent boys will occasionally find a stain on their underwear in the mornings as the only evidence of this nighttime ejaculation. Like erections, these "wet dreams" are also perfectly normal, and are a way for your body to release extra semen that has been produced in your testicles. Your father will be able to explain all this to you in more detail.

## FEMALE MATURITY

A girl's body goes through even more complex changes than those of a boy, because it has to prepare for the very complex job of becoming a mother. One of the first physical changes unique to adolescent girls is the growth of their breasts. This growth begins as small, soft lumps under each nipple. Over a period of months, these lumps gradually increase in size and shape. Eventually, your breasts will develop to a point where, if you become pregnant, they will be capable of producing milk to nurse your newborn baby.

During adolescent development, your breasts may occasionally become sore. This soreness often happens at the same time as menstruation, and is a normal part of womanhood. You may also feel some self-consciousness about the size of your breasts (as in too large, too small, or not shaped just right). Remember that your body is unique — different from everyone else on earth. The contour of your breasts is a God-given quality that no person can justifiably criticize. It is a beauty that is yours alone.

You will also notice some increase in the size of your labia. The labia are the two folds of skin (sometimes called "lips") on either side of the opening into your vagina. At the top of your vaginal opening is a small lump called the clitoris. Occasionally your clitoris will become firm, swollen, or tingly feeling for a few minutes at a time. This is perfectly normal.

Menstruation is probably the most significant physical change that takes place during female adolescence. Usually somewhere between 10 and 12 years of age, girls begin to have cramping sensations in their pelvic area. In the beginning, these cramps are only sporadic, but with time they become stronger. Then, girls begin to notice a little bleeding from their vagina close to the same time as the cramping. Over a period of months, the quantity of bleeding gradually increases in amount.

Where is this blood coming from? Above, we discussed the fact that a woman's ovaries produce one egg each month. That egg cell travels from the ovary into the uterus, where it lies in the uterine lining and awaits the arrival of sperm to create a new baby, but if sperm do not appear within a few days, the egg and the inside lining of the uterus will peel off. They will then be carried out of the uterus and into the vagina by a small flow of blood. It usually takes about three to five days for the flow to stop, and during this time a woman wears one of a variety of cloth pads to absorb the blood. This monthly flow is called "menstruation."

Girls often feel concerns, and even fears, about menstruation, and understandably so! Bleeding and painful cramps are usually signs that a person should go see the doctor, but menstruation is completely natural, just like breathing and sleeping. It's the way you were designed — an intimate part of being a woman. Be sure to talk with your mother more about this subject. She'll be happy that you trust her enough to ask.

## WHO PUT THE BRAKES ON?

For me (Joe), it seemed like the only thing that mattered during my turbulent teenage years were sports and girls, but endless hours lifting weights couldn't produce enough muscles to impress my coaches. Neither could endless hours in front of the mirror trying to find a cool hairstyle to impress the girls of my junior high school. I asked myself, why did my friend Paul get muscles sooner? Why did he run so much faster? Why was Susie Brown attracted to him and not to me? I questioned whether there was something wrong with my body!

Occasionally, a boy or girl does not physically mature as quickly as his or her peers. This can cause terrible feelings of inferiority or embarrassment. The onset of physical development is normally accompanied by some uneasiness, but when that development is delayed for too long, the uneasiness can become overwhelming.

Surely you've noticed that some boys are still short and rather hairless, while most others their own age are tall and muscular. Or, you've seen female teens whose figures are still girl-like, while their peers are developing curves in all the natural places.

If you are not developing as quickly as you'd expect, you may begin to question, "What's wrong with me?" But don't worry. Your body is entirely unique. Your pituitary gland is on its own schedule — one that is different from every other person on earth. In time, the physical changes you've been anticipating will happen to you, too. Tell your parents about your feelings. They will understand, and can help you deal with your doubts or fears.

I (Joe) remember two dark-haired boys named Jerry Bus and Herbert Hearn who developed hair, muscles, speed, and good looks two years before I did. The girls "dug their socks off," and these guys were our football team's biggest heroes. My anxiety would have decreased greatly if I would have known at that time that some boys who mature rapidly also stop maturing sooner, and that slower developing boys, like me, actually catch up with them and often pass them up in high school or college.

My oldest son Brady is handsome at six feet, three inches tall. He's built like a body-builder, plays guitar, and sings the songs he writes to amazed high school and college audiences, but Brady was not that way in the beginning. During grades four through seven, Brady was often depressed because his body was so awkward and unfit for basketball. He thought life would never be a happy experience. Little did Brady realize the potential that rested inside his developing body. It just took some time to come out.

Consider a tiny acorn, how it can grow into a huge tree and produce enough lumber to build an entire room. Or think about an apple seed and how many thousands of apples it can reproduce. Your body is like that acorn, like that small seed. In time, it will begin to develop like you've never imagined!

If you know people who seem to be lagging behind their peers in development, then do your best to be a true friend to them. Kids often tease those who are smaller and less physically mature than they are. This form of teasing can be extremely damaging to one's self-esteem, but encouraging words from friends like you can be just the fuel to help get them by until physical development kicks in.

## WHAT DO YOU THINK?

- What sort of physical changes have you noticed about yourself recently?
- How do you feel about these changes happening to you?

**Nicholas Comninellis & Joe White**

- What questions do you have about sexuality? Who do you trust to talk to about these?
- Do you have a friend who is not developing as quickly as other people? What could you say or do to help encourage this person?

## FOR TEEN EYES ONLY

The physical makeover that occurs during adolescence is nothing short of miraculous. Amazing biological changes within will transform you in the space of a few short years, from a child into a person with a fully adult body.

King David of ancient Israel was aware of some of the marvelous ways God designed our bodies to change and mature. He wrote of God:

> You made all the delicate inner part of my body, and knit them together in my mother's womb. Thank you for making me so wonderfully complex. It is amazing to think about. Your workmanship is marvelous — and how well I know it (Ps. 139:13–15; Living Bible).

Your body is beautiful, intricate, and has fantastic potential within. Be happy with the physical changes that are taking place inside of you! They are both amazing and an integral part of the plan God has for your life — one that will lead to deep happiness and lasting success.

"**God really does**
care for me!"

**9** **Nine Things**
**Countdown to Adolescence**

# Chapter

**9**

# Search for
# Self-Esteem

## GETTING TO THE CORE

Teenagers are complex. Many issues are important to them, including several we've already touched on, but if we could put our finger on the number one felt need of people like you, it would be simply this: The desire to feel good about yourself — the need for self-esteem, for an excellent self-image.

With all the changes going on, adolescence is a time filled with feelings of vulnerability. You ask yourself, "Do I look all right? Will my friends accept me? Will my parents agree with my plans? Do I have the talent to succeed in school or music or sports?"

For the next several years your need for self-esteem will be at an all time high. Josh McDowell, a popular author and speaker among high school and college students, correctly points out:

Persons with a good, healthy sense of self-worth feel significant. They believe that they matter, even that the world is a better place because they are there. Such persons can interact with others and appreciate their worth, too. They radiate hope, joy, and trust. They are alive to their feelings. They accept themselves as delightful to God — a ship moving forward confidently, under full sail.[1]

If you feel good about yourself, you will naturally perform better, experience more successes, and draw the healthy attention of others. If you feel poorly about yourself, as Josh continues to explain, just the opposite is likely to occur:

An inadequate self-image robs us of the energy and powers of attention to relate to others because we are absorbed with our own inadequacies. That is especially true when we're in the presence of people who remind us of our shortcomings. . . . In such situations we are so self-conscious that we cannot give sufficient attention to others. As a result we may be regarded as being either uncaring or proud. Our feelings of inadequacy prevent us from reaching out to love and care for others. . . .

Persons with an inadequate self-image look to other people's opinions, praise, or criticisms as determining factors in how they feel or think about themselves at a particular moment.

Persons with a poor sense of self-worth are slaves to the opinions of others. They are not free to be themselves.[2]

## FORMULAS FOR FAILURE

People will do almost anything to acquire this elusive self-esteem — even things that they know are foolish. So if drugs, dangerous stunts, or sexual escapades seem to create good feelings — even if only for a moment — they may just give them a try.

Less extreme but just as deceiving, many teens (and adults, too!) attempt to find their self-esteem through improving the way they look. Most teenagers feel dissatisfied with their physical attractiveness. Girls often sense they are too tall. Boys frequently feel too short. Some kids believe they are too fat or too skinny. Some think they have too many freckles or their lips are too large. Others figure they have too few dimples, or their nose is too small, feet too big, chin too prominent, thighs too large, eyebrows too bushy, ears too flat, shoulders too sloping. The list is almost endless, but no matter how you try to buff your body, the fact is that it will never completely satisfy you.

Teenagers also try to find their self-esteem through money and possessions. The kid who comes from a family with all the "right" stuff (huge house, fast car, patio, and pool) is more likely to think he or she is really somebody. Likewise, if the teen has some spending money and can afford to go shopping whenever, the tendency is to feel like "I've arrived!" When money is lacking at home, and one

**Nicholas Comninellis & Joe White**

doesn't have the clothes, bikes, cars, videos, computers, or CD collections of more wealthy friends, feelings of inadequacy and low self-esteem usually run rampant.

Another frequent strategy for finding self-esteem is through getting in good with the popular kids, or at least some group where you feel accepted. This can indeed help you feel great about yourself, but as we discussed in chapter 4, true friends are often hard to come by, and many peers are only looking for how they themselves can benefit from a friendship with you; not how the two of you can make each other stronger and happier.

### Formula for Success

Want to feel good about yourself? Want some surefire plans for a great self-image? We're about to share with you a formula for personal growth and success that year after year has inspired literally millions of young people around the world. Why is it so popular? Because it works!

This formula was clearly demonstrated in the life of a 12-year-old boy in ancient Israel. His name was Jesus Christ. Luke, a physician, noted that, "Jesus grew in wisdom and stature, and in favor with God and men" (Luke 2:52; NIV). In this single phrase is wrapped up all the important areas of personal growth for the teenage years:

Wisdom = Emotional and intellectual
     development
Stature = Physical growth and training
Favor with God = Spiritual maturity
Favor with men = Growth in social abilities

As you develop in each of these areas, you'll become a more complete person, and that completeness will provide a very reliable, healthy source of self-esteem. You see, self esteem is ultimately up to you. It's not about how handsome or pretty you are on the outside. That which is in your heart is what really counts. Self-esteem is not about the wealth of your family. The world is filled with well-to-do, but terribly unhappy teenagers. Neither is lasting self-esteem a quality you can get from your friends. You should not allow anyone to have so much control over you. Rather than all of this, self-esteem is something you can only earn for yourself. Let's look at how to develop each of these four areas:

• **Wisdom**

Now is the perfect time in life to learn all you can about the good in the world. Your classes in school and conversations with your family will expose you to enormous, and sometimes challenging new ideas. Take full advantage of these. Read all you can. Enroll in tough classes, and as you do so, remember there is more to wisdom than just filling yourself up with new information. Wisdom also means learning to distinguish the pros and the cons, what is better or worse, right or wrong about each idea.

This process is called critical thinking. Conversation with others is one of the best ways to develop your own ability to evaluate the rightness or usefulness of what you're learning. So engage your teachers, parents, and friends. Ask the hard questions. Do the research. Find the

**Nicholas Comninellis & Joe White**

elusive answers. You will feel better about yourself, and with good reason!

• **Stature**

One of the most exciting parts of adolescence is all the new physical abilities that come along with it. You can run faster, jump farther, hit harder, dance more gracefully, and shoot more accurately. Not only this, but your school and community also give you more opportunities for athletic performance and competition than ever before.

Let none of these pass you by! Try out for a variety of activities and discover which sports you're good at and enjoy the most. Train yourself to be the very best of athletes, excelling in strength, endurance, skill, attitude, and teamwork. Press on to make physical fitness not simply a teenage pastime, but also a lifestyle you can take with you into adulthood.

• **Favor with God**

Each person has profound questions within. How did life begin? Where did the universe come from? Is there really an absolute right or wrong? How do I tell the difference? What is God like? What happens after I die?

Often, the more profound the questions, the less likely people are to actually discuss them, but rather than ignore these critical questions, seek out the answers. Talk to your parents. Quiz your church leaders. Read your Bible. Get close to Jesus. You will find the answers, and your entire life will begin to shine. Get a glimpse of Jesus' incredible affection for you, and you can't help but justifiably feel great about who you are!

• **Favor with men**

Good relationships can bring incredible happiness to your life, but the necessary social skills to build these relationships don't always come naturally. Instead, these skills must be discovered and polished. Becoming a good friend can really take work. It demands learning to choose companions carefully, to share your feelings, to ask for advice, to listen with interest, and to work as a team. Add some of that commitment love to your friendships and then watch how incredibly warm and close you can become with each other. The work will definitely pay off!

## FOURFOLD MATURITY

Growing and developing in each of these areas — mentally, physically, spiritually, and socially — will do wonders for your confidence and ability to enjoy life to the max. Your goal should be to become as complete and healthy a person as possible. Set goals for yourself in each of these four areas. Start working toward your own progress. The sooner you do, the sooner you'll begin feeling better about who you are.

Each of these four areas, of course, is interrelated. The disciplines of focus and endurance you learn in athletics, for example, will help you become a better student. Your intellectual brightness will also help you to win athletic competitions. As you develop in one area, the others will be positively affected as well. Growing like this is a process and takes time. Be patient, stay determined, and you will see yourself become more like the person of your dreams.

Elizabeth did it. As a 15 year old at Liberty High School, she wrote:

> The older I grow, the more pressure I have to face. It would be easy to join a crowd of people smoking or drinking, or to have sex and use foul language. However, I made a conscious decision, early on, not to take the easy road, and it was the best decision I have ever made. It has allowed me to be myself and to make my own choices.

> Every morning I start by spending time with God. I devote my first efforts to Jesus. I make sure to set my priorities and He is always first. I know that I am loved, even on days when I feel no one cares. I know Jesus loves me. If it were not for the relationship I have with Him, I would not be the person I am today.

> Throughout my adolescent years, I have been given many opportunities because of the right decisions I made. I go to school, I turn in my homework on time, and make good grades. I play sports and I'm involved in music. I do what I love to do, and learn to enjoy what others might consider boring.

> I never wish to go to wild parties nor do I worry about the opinions of others, because I know most of the people who look confident and drive nice cars are hurting and empty. Every person is on a search to find purpose and security.

It takes some people a lifetime to find true self-worth, and some never find it.

I find my security first in my faith, then in friends I know I can trust. I stay involved in activities that will build me physically and emotionally. The advice I have based my life on is to take every opportunity and never pass up the chance to be myself. I am exactly the way God meant me to be.

You, too, can be exactly the way God meant you to be! Like Elizabeth, you, too, can enjoy the confidence and satisfaction that radiates from a life that is fully developing. The choice is up to you. Decide for yourself, and get growing!

## Esteem-Building Routine

An athlete must work out almost every day to stay in shape. A musician will improve only with constant practice. Similarly, your self-esteem will grow faster when some essential rules are followed:

**• Focus on what is important in the long run.**

The world we live in will get you to believe (if you listen long enough) that all that matters is how you look, how much money you have, or how popular you are, but ask the Miss America who's grown wrinkled, or the ex-pro athlete who can't run anymore how important those things really are. They will both tell you to develop inner beauty, discipline, and personal relationships — virtues that continue to be important, regardless of your age.

**Nicholas Comninellis & Joe White**

• **Concentrate on your strengths.**

While you are young, explore all the areas of life you possibly can. You will probably discover some hidden talent or interest you were never aware of — one that could become a lifelong hobby or even your career track. As you discover your greatest strengths, focus on developing these. Sure, you will occasionally be attracted by some other pursuit or pastime, but the happiest people are usually those who identify early and make the most of what they do best.

• **Think positive!**

Focus on the good things you see in yourself, and quit beating yourself up over your flaws and over the mistakes you've made. Post your successes in huge letters on the bulletin board of your mind; signs that say things like these:

> "God really does care for me!"
> "I resisted temptation today."
> "I'm getting better!"
> "I can do it!"

Rip down the old dusty signs that say "I'm no good," "No one likes me," or "I can never forgive myself for that." When you start to get down on yourself, just check out what's on the bulletin board of your mind and keep posted only the good stuff!

• **Remember, pain leads to gain!**

In the last 30 years I (Joe) have been able to work with well over 100,000 athletes, from Pop Warner to Super

Bowl and World Series MVPs. The only thing that all truly great athletes have in common is scars. That's right, scars. On their knees, shoulders, ankles, elbows, chins, noses, and . . . emotions. Every aspiring athlete, scholar, and friend-maker has a personal road map literally filled with milestones marked by personal failure. I failed repeatedly as a kid. I was lonely, felt ugly, was ridiculed by friends, rejected by girls, sat on the bench, and in general walked through the valley of failure for years.

All four of my own kids experienced extensive brokenness as they "increased in wisdom and stature and favor with God and man." Like my friends who played in Super Bowls and All Star games, we all kept getting up again, dusting ourselves off, and jumping back into the game, time after time. Scars aren't defeats — they're just tests. They build character. They make you stronger. They give you compassion for others in pain. They will become your friends, and propel you toward success.

Ultimately, self-esteem is not simply about "feeling good." By itself, feeling good is hollow. Rather, healthy self-esteem is about actually becoming a solid, complete individual through and through, regardless of how high or low you feel on any particular day. By developing your mind, body, spirit, and social skills — by focusing on what's important, on your strengths, on positive thoughts, and turning pain into gain — you will nurture an incredible sense of happiness with who you are, and rightly so!

- Why is it important to feel good about yourself? What sort of benefits does it bring?
- What are the consequences of a poor self-image?
- What is a sure-fire formula for a good self-image?
- What's your relationship with God like? How can you make it better?
- Why is it helpful to concentrate on your strengths instead of your weaknesses?
- How can obstacles and failures actually make you stronger?

## FOR TEEN EYES ONLY

In this book we've explored the hardest, most challenging parts of adolescence, but don't get the wrong idea that everything will be this way. On the contrary, you are entering the most wonderful years of your life to date. You are about to make fascinating discoveries about the world. You're on the brink of incredible friendships like you've never known. You're about to experience new feelings, new forces, and new freedoms.

Yes, there will be challenges, but challenges can make your life even stronger. Creating a diamond requires 1,000,000 pounds of pressure per square inch, and 5,000 degrees of heat. The process may turn ordinary graphite into pulverized powder, but with care and attention, a lovely and priceless jewel can be the result.

Likewise, take advantage of the pressures and heat you experience during the teenage years. Like the creation of a diamond, they will help you become strong and pure.

**Notes**

1. Josh McDowell, *Building Your Self-Image* (Wheaton, IL: Living Books, 1978), p. 24.
2. Ibid., p. 24–25.

# DARWIN'S DEMISE

## JOE WHITE AND
## NICHOLAS COMNINELLIS

*Amazing facts and
information showing
the fallacies of evolution
presented in a format
appealing to teens and
young adults*

- The quantity of complex information stored in a pinhead's volume of DNA is equivalent to the content of a pile of paperback books spanning the distance from earth to the moon 500 times.

- The human eye can handle 1.5 million simultaneous messages.

- A single drop of blood can be delivered anywhere in the body within 20 seconds.

*Darwin's Demise* is a hard-hitting, fast-moving collection of evidence for creation presented in an interesting and entertaining format for young adults. What is the evidence for creation? Why is evolution so appealing? What have we learned over the last century? Here are the cold, hard facts and the ultimate conclusion is that there is indeed a Creator.

White has devoted his life to ministering to youth, while Comninellis shares insight from biochemistry and physiology into the origin of life.

6 x 9 trade paper • 192 pages • $12.99
ISBN-13: 978-0-89051-352-1 • ISBN-10: 0-89051-352-X

*Available at Christian bookstores nationwide*

# WHERE DO I GO FROM HERE?

### NICHOLAS COMNINELLIS

*Stories of young adults who made great decisions —
and the dramatic outcomes*

- Excellent guide for those who are facing big choices
- Explains how to focus on the right motives behind life decisions
- Teaches how to make wise decisions
- Advice is biblically founded
- Perfect gift for graduates

Life is full of decisions — both major and minor. Should I take this job? Should I go to college? What if he asks me to marry him? This book is especially aimed at young people and their decision-making processes. Its goal is to help young people become more effective by focusing on the right motives, looking ahead to potential outcomes, and ultimately turning to Jesus Christ for guidance. A beautiful gift book full of vignettes of young people faced with decisions, and how they tackled each one.

7 x 7 hardcover • 112 pages • $11.99
ISBN-13: 978-0-89221-515-7 • ISBN-10: 0-89221-515-1

*Available at Christian bookstores nationwide*

# THE AUTHORS

Dr. Joe White is the president of Kanakuk Kamps in Branson, Missouri, whose 12 locations in the Ozarks and Colorado provide athletic training and spiritual guidance to over 27,000 teenagers each summer. Joe is a frequent guest speaker at national meetings including Promise Keepers, and the author of 13 books, including *Faith Training* and *Pure Excitement* (winner of the Gold Medallion Book of the Year Award) and *Life Training*. Joe and his wife, Debbie Jo, have four adult children.

Nicholas Comninellis is an associate professor of family medicine and public health at the University of Missouri-Kansas City. In 2003, he formed INMED — the Institute for International Medicine, which prepares health professionals for the rigors of serving in medical missions. He is also part of the medical ministry of Kalukembe Hospital and the Lubango Evangelical Medical Center, both in central Angola, Africa. During the summer, he serves on the medical staff at Kanakuk Kamps in Branson, Missouri. The father of three teens himself, Nicholas is also the author of five books, including *Where Do I Go From Here? — Making the Right Decisions in Life* (New Leaf Press, 2002), and *Darwin's Demise* (Master Books, 2001) with Dr. Joe White. Nicholas lives in Liberty, Missouri, where he is part of Shoal Creek Community Church. For more information, go to www.creativeenergy.org.